LIFE DESIGN BLUEPRINTS PLAYBOOK

A step-by-step guide to your ideal life.

Dr. Susan R. Meyer, Life Architect

Table of Contents

Creating Your Blueprint

Creating Your Blueprint

When you work with an architect to create or modify a building, you may use the past as prologue to the future. You may think about buildings you love or admire. If you are designing a home, you may be thinking about elements of your childhood home that you loved – or hated. You will think about what works well for you and what doesn't. From this, the architect will craft a design or blueprint for the project.

Similarly, as you create a blueprint for your life, you may want to look back and evaluate who you are and what has worked well or not so well in the past. Chapter 2,   Who Are You? Will help you do this. In Chapter 3, Vision, Goals and Legacy, you will have the opportunity to develop an overall framework for your ideal life. This is similar to creating the frame for a house. How many rooms will there be? How will they relate to each other?

Each of the subsequent chapters represents a different room in your house, or a separate area of your life that might need some attention. Some areas may require major change; some a bit of tweaking; some are perfect the way they are. Pick and choose.

Chapter 4, Nurturing, addresses the need for love and attention in everyone. It helps you look at how strong your need to nurture is, how that plays out, and how you are nurtured by others. Chapter 5, Relationships, is similar, but broadens out to help you define both how you want to relate to friends and family and how many or few relationships are ideal for you. The need to be productive is strong in most people. Chapter 6, Meaningful Work, helps you to explore paid employment and volunteer work that fits your ideal lifestyle and adds meaning to your life. In Chapter 7, Spirituality, you will be presented with a broader view of what spirituality means and how to nurture your inner being. Not finding space for self-expression?

Chapter 8, Creativity and Self-Expression discusses how creativity keeps us young and vibrant and offers options for discovering your talents. Finally, because taking care of yourself is essential to your ideal life, Chapter 9, Health and Wellness, offers suggestions for remaining vibrant.

Some chapters will call you immediately. Some may be areas you will want to visit later. There's no special order to the topics except for starting with Chapter 3. I often advise clients to return to Chapter 3 and revisit their goals after they've completed the rest of the process to see if their goals have changed.

I've used parts of this process very successfully with a wide range of people over the past twenty years. I wish that same success for each of you.

Who Are You?

Who Are You?

Researching Your Own History

Blueprints are for all of you who have spent years chasing dreams, only to find yourself still at square one, still longing after the unreachable, and still unhappy. They are plans for defining your goals and reaching them, and remaining reasonably sane, satisfied and fulfilled along the way.

Many books offer you someone else's solutions to making your life better in some way. Often, the path shown is to improvement as the author thinks you should be – usually based on his or her life experience. I am proposing something very different here. I am not offering you our answers to your questions. I am showing you how to look to your own experience – your own life – for the answers.

I plan to guide you on a journey through your own life. I think that by writing your life history, looking at where you've been and what you've done and by dreaming a little about your future, you will be able to create your own best path.

Some women spend their whole lives chasing after dreams they haven't created – being the person their parents-teachers-lovers-husbands thought they should be. Their heads are full of "shoulds" they are too busy trying to live up to some impossible ideals to actually let go and enjoy their lives. Maybe it's time for a different approach. Is it time to lower your expectations? Learn how to find happiness in small things. Live each day to the fullest, no matter where you are on your path.

Don't wait for someone else to tell you what's right for you. Make up your own rules for how you will live your life. Plan for your own future, but don't dwell on it. Once your plan is in place, let life take over; leave room for unexpected and wonderful surprises. Remember, this is a Blueprint process – and blueprints can always be changed.

Learn to distinguish between what you want and what you need. Learn how to become financially independent so that you are no longer a slave to that paycheck or those credit cards. Have multiple career plans – find as many paths as possible to what you want. Learn how to make your own combination of activities that contribute to a fuller, richer life.

Life History as Blueprint Background

Creating a life history is a little like thinking about all the places you've lived or visited before you meet with the architect to plan your new house. For many of us, our ideal house – and our ideal life – is made up of bits and pieces we're collected along the way. Think of this process as creating a collage that will help you see more clearly what you want next.

In most planning processes, you begin by looking at where you are now, but I believe that there's more to creating Life Blueprints than that. Before you plan a new residence, you might want to be very clear about what you have enjoyed in old residences. Similarly, before you decide where you are going, you ought to know how you got to where you are now. What people and events contributed to making you the person you are today? How have the patterns of your life shaped how you think and what you do? What do you want to carry forward? What do you want to leave behind? And, maybe most important, what have you forgotten? How many of life's important lessons are hidden in the depths of your mind? It's time to find out.

Logistics

You are about to turn autobiographer and write the history of your life. It may sound like an enormous project, but once you get started, you may be amazed at how much you have to say and how quickly you can say it. First, you'll need to create an atmosphere or tone. The right props go far towards making the most reluctant of us into prolific writers.

Your first big decision in writing your life history is whether you are a pen and paper person or a computer person. It doesn't matter what your choice is; it does matter that you are entirely comfortable. I composed my life history primarily on the computer, but I also carried notebooks at all times so that I could revise and add pieces.

If you will be using a computer, unless you live alone and no one ever touches your computer, you might want to have a flash drive to store your material or are using a password. Your life history, unless you later decide to share, is for your eyes only. If you are working on a computer, you probably know that whatever can go wrong will go wrong, so the flash drive can also serve as your back-up copy. You are about to do a lot of work, and I don't want you to leave anything to chance. Find your favorite font – you'll be looking at this a lot, so if appearance is important, you might as Ill be looking at something that you enjoy.

If you will be using pen and paper, think about what writing materials you are most comfortable with. You may want to indulge in a little bit of luxury here, but you will need to be sure that you are not sacrificing convenience for luxury. For instance, I really love good leather. It was tempting to buy a beautiful (and expensive) leather-bound notebook for this project. The idea of a beautiful fountain pen was tempting too. In fact, I own several of them. Here's where practicality won out, though. Fountain pens are wonderful, but if you write, pause, write a little more, pause some more, your pen is sure to dry up. Leather-bound tomes look beautiful, but they weigh a lot. If you are on the go, how much extra weight do you want to tote?

Shop around a little. Handle pens until you find the right one for you. It should write smoothly and feel comfortable in your hand. Experiment with fine points and broad points, with roller balls and ball points. Try different colors. Maybe you want a multi-color history. Try pencils. You may find out that this is your implement of choice.

Look at different kinds of notebooks and pads, too. There are countless options in stationary, business supply and art stores and even more at your neighborhood discount store or pharmacy. If you plan to work on your life history a little bit at a time – as I did – be sure that your choice fits into whatever you usually carry. Just under 9" x 7" fits into most pocketbooks.

When you have your materials, try to decide when you can most easily carve out some time for this project. Once you get started, you can probably do a little bit of work whenever you can squeeze in a few minutes or whenever an idea comes to you, but at the beginning, it is best if you carve out some quiet time. Find a place where you can work without disturbances of any kind for at least 30 minutes. An hour would be better. Let the machine answer the telephone. Find your favorite radio station, tape or CD – something that sets a tone.

There is no "right" music. Different parts of your life history might require a different tone – meditative – reflective – energizing – nostalgic – they all work. One day you might want opera; the next you might need to sing along with moldy oldies or folk favorites.

Now that you are (finally) ready to write, sit down and begin. You can start anywhere, meander around, go back and forth – whatever keeps you writing. One event may bring another seemingly unrelated experience to mind. Don't censor! Don't stop! You can go back and organize later on. The organization presented below is not meant to be anything but general suggestions. Please don't feel that you must include or limit yourself to these topics!

Organizing Your Life History

Since this is a voyage of exploration, there are very few markers. There are a few things that you probably will want to at least consider in reviewing your life. If some of these topics don't apply to you, ignore them. If some are painful, try to come back to them. If you absolutely can't write about any of these areas, try to ask yourself why and record your response.

This is not therapy and it is not sharing. Everything here is for you alone. Although I will share with you some ways to organize the information about your life, I don't know each of you personally, so I would not presume to interpret.

Family

What do you remember about your grandparents? Were they (or other older relatives) a significant factor in how you Ire raised? Did they shape your values or role expectations?

Describe your parents. How did they spend their time? How were you raised? What are some significant incidents that give a clear picture of how you related to your parents?

Who was in your immediate circle when you were growing up? Was it just the nuclear family (mom, dad, kids, pets) or did you have an extended family (grandparents or other adults in the house, cousins or other relatives so nearby that you were almost always together). How did this influence your values or attitudes? How did you relate to/interact with these people?

Childhood Markers, School

What were some of the marker events, or most significant incidents in your childhood?
What kind of school did you go to? How did you do in school? How did you feel about school? What were your favorites? What did you dislike? What were your successes? Your failures?

Did you go on to higher education? Why or why not?

If you did go to college, describe your college experiences. Who was important to you? What were your successes? Your failures? Did – how did – college shape your post-school decisions?

Work

Where did you live when you finished school? Why? How old were you? What were your plans?

What is the first thing you remember wanting to do when you grew up? If this changed, when and how? If you could be that thing now, would you?

Describe your work history. Don't forget to include work inside the home. Yes, raising a family counts! You used countless skills to do this.

For each work experience – paid or unpaid, full or part-time – describe how you felt about the work. Describe how you felt about yourself as a worker.

Relationships

Chronicle your social life. Who are your friends? How long have they been friends? What links you to them? How do you spend your time together.

Describe your romantic life. Who has been important to you? Why? How long did each relationship last? Did you marry or make a long term commitment to another person?

Leisure

How do you spend your free time? What kinds of activities do you enjoy? Are they individual or group activities? Are you involved in any sports? Active in a gym? Take yoga or other classes?

Spirit

What is your religious background? Were you actively involved in religious activities as a child? Has this changed in adulthood? Do you still practice your faith of origin or have you switched or stopped? How do you satisfy your spiritual needs? Formally or informally? Alone or with others?

This list is a starting point. Write as much as you can, then go back and write some more. If you are over 30, you should have the equivalent of at least 20 typed pages – more than twice that number in a handwritten document.

Organizing Your Life History: Personal Patterns

Now that you've done the hardest part of the job – writing about your life – you will want to look back over the trip and understand how you came to the ground you're standing on today. You will be using the tools in this Blueprint to organize and categorize your life history. You are, in effect, comparing the blueprints from previous dwellings to the new structure you are about to create. Your preferences will govern the shape and size of the rooms. Your patterns of behavior will help show you the logical flow for the new structure. All of this will make it easier for you to complete your Goals Blueprint and all the other Blueprints that will help you create your ideal future.

This Blueprint shows you how to analyze your operating plan to date, pinpointing decision points in the life history and tracing choices. Your analysis will serve as a roadmap to your new life plan. It will help you have a clearer view of patterns that serve you well and those that may hold you back. You'll do this by dividing your experiences into a series of segments that we'll call blocks.

Life is made up of a series of building blocks. These blocks represent the relationship between our experiences and our belief system. We pile these blocks one on top of the other to create the pattern that is our lives. Sometimes, though, the pattern is not what we expected. This may be true because we so rarely look at the construction that is our lives.

When a bricklayer constructs a wall, he carefully examines his materials. He looks over each brick to be sure that it is true – no cracks, not warped in any way, of the same color and construction as the other bricks that will make up the wall. Then he carefully mixes the ingredients to make the mortar that will hold the bricks together. If the ingredients are not in balance, the mortar will be too thin and not hold or will dry and crack. The bricks will not stay in place. Carefully, very carefully, the bricklayer puts just the right amount of mortar on the trowel, then gently taps the brick in place, smoothing away the excess, making sure the brick is aligned with the others – not too far forward, not too far back. If only we could build the walls of our own lives with such care!

Unfortunately, we don't always have this luxury. Our lives develop – often without much attention paid to the construction or the materials. Some of the bricks may be faulty. Some may really be bars of gold. In examining our life histories, you are, in effect, looking at each of the bricks in your walls. Some may be perfect; some may need to be replaced. Part of the work you will be doing in this Blueprint is reviewing the basic constructs – the bricks – that make up your life to date. This experience may be exhilarating or painful or both.

Don't expect to move through the exercises in this Blueprint quickly. Sometimes, answers may flow quickly. Other times, you may not be able to write at all. Move away from the material when you need to. Often, your mind will keep working through the questions in the background and answers will emerge while you are busy doing something else. Remember that you have no deadlines, and the journey will be worth it. After all, you're worth the effort! Your work will have a tremendous payoff. By the time you have finished, you will have a much clearer picture of who you are and what basic thoughts, or underlying assumptions have governed the decisions you have made to date.

Triumph!

As you move forward in the examination of your life that you started by writing your life history – as you use that life history as a map of your past and your future – you will need to put up a series of signposts. The first signposts that you erect will mark your triumphs.

This is often very hard for some people. Why is it that we can remember every mistake we ever made but our successes just seem to slip away from us? Some of the most successful people I have ever met have spoken about feeling like an imposter. There are dozens of books on the subject. "If they really knew who I am …." Maybe, just maybe, they do know! Maybe we don't know who we are. Maybe we don't recognize our own successes.

It's time to put all modesty and need for perfection aside now and chronicle all of your achievements. If you are working with a handwritten document, pick up a brightly colored marker or pen. If you are using a computer file, go into symbols and find something vivid and cheerful or simply change the color of the text. If you use a symbol, make it large and put it on the clipboard so that you can copy it into your document often.

Exercise 1 – Identify your successes

What you need: your life history

color - markers, type color

or symbols (computer)

What you will do: mark all your life successes

Why you will do   To have a clear record of your

this: achievements

To link your feelings to your

achievements

Start reading through your life history. Read slowly and carefully. You are looking for your successes. Mark them all. In fact, you may also have to do some more writing here. As you reread your life, think of it, for the moment, as the life of a stranger. What do you admire most about this person? How did she handle the events you are reading about? Don't you wish you could have done that? Whoops – wait a minute – you did do that! Until you see it written down, you may have no idea of all the things that you have done well, all the obstacles you have overcome, all the people you have influenced. Now is the time for you – finally – to be impressed with yourself.

As you read each incident that makes up your life history, concentrate on the evidence of success. If, as you read, you realize that you have glossed over an event, write more. If this is handwritten, just mark the section and page number. Write in "see the appendix" or some other indicator that will work for you and remind you to flip to the back of the book. If you are using a computer, just insert more information. Remember – no false modesty here. Once you've identified your successes, you'll be looking at how you felt at the time.

Exercise 2 – Feelings about success

What you need: Your marked life history

Markers (hard copy) or symbols
(computer)

A new file or notebook section

What you will do: Review each success to identify
the emotions related to the
experience

Why you will do
this: To link your feelings to your
achievements

When you have finished marking and writing, you will be creating a new file or notebook section for the next step. Go back over every success that you marked and answer the following questions:

Part 1. How was I feeling about myself at the beginning of this experience?

Why are you answering this? Who cares? You do! Remember – your purpose here is to learn from

31

your successes so that you can repeat them. Your emotional state, whether you realize it or not, had some influence on the actions you took. How can you learn to use your emotions if you can't identify them?

As women, we may not have been taught the harmful idea that so many men are asked to believe – that emotions should be separated from action. Intuitively, we understand the importance of context and of emotions in understanding our actions – or at least we once did.

Bettina Aptheker, in *Tapestries of Life*, summarizes a short story by Susan Glaspell, in which a group of women immediately understand that their neighbor murdered her husband – and why – while the sheriff remains baffled. The women read the emotional signs in the room, none of which are visible to the men. As one, they see their sister's act as justified and remain mute. How can we deny or ignore this gift? But, in our need to keep up with a hectic and often callous world, we turn our back on these strengths.

If you have lost touch with your emotional context, this is a good time to begin flexing those intuitive muscles. Reach deep inside you! It's still there! Reclaim your emotions and understand exactly how they work for you. This is a big part of owning – being fully in touch with – all aspects of your own life. Recognize that no one ever operates in a vacuum. You are part of a universe rich in hopes, dreams, fantasies, and feelings as well as actions. Which of these have guided you to make the right choice?

Part 2. ***If I was experiencing negative emotions, what did I do to use them in a positive way OR what did I do to work through them or get beyond them?***

For example: Frankie has a real fear of not having enough money. She's afraid she'll die old, alone, and on the streets with a shopping cart. (A fear many other women share!) She translates that fear into the drive that makes her one of the most persistent saleswomen you'll ever meet. She's not a bulldog, but she keeps coming back and she keeps trying because every "no" is a rag in the bag lady's shopping bag and every "yes" is another payment on the coop. Her fear doesn't hold her back or paralyze her, it drives her to success.

Were you afraid? What did that feel like? How clearly can you identify your fear? In what ways did being afraid stop or limit your actions? Did you make choices based on what was safest? Were you unable to make a choice? How long did that last? If you worked through your fear, how were you able to do this? Did you develop a technique that you were able to transfer to other situations?

Annie is afraid of death. Sometimes, she wakes up in the middle of the night paralyzed with fear. Over time, she realized that she would have to find a way to cope with her fear or she'd never be able to go on with her life. She decided that if she

34

was dead, either she wouldn't have any consciousness at all, so she wouldn't be able to worry, or the next life would be wonderful, so she'd have nothing to worry about. Either way, there was nothing she could do now and there would be nothing to actually worry about when the moment came. This may sound simplistic to you, but it works very well for her. Even though the fear comes back every so often, she repeats this chain of reasoning and the fear lifts.

Kelly used to obsess all the time. She was unable to get anything done because she was always catastrophizing. She also developed a habit of rubbing her hands against the front of her jeans until they became threadbare. Finally, she had had enough. She trained herself to have obsession breaks. She would give in to her obsessive fears for five minutes – no longer – and then move on to some concrete activity.

Part 3. If I was experiencing a positive emotion, what was it? How did I use it?

Patsy is an actress. She feels a real adrenaline rush every time she walks out on stage. She knows that she could fail, but she gets high on the risk. It gives her an edge. It keeps her crisp. Every performance is a new beginning; a challenge. And every night, she's a star.

Sally gets real joy from teaching. Every time she sees that someone in the group grasped a new concept, she's thrilled. She uses the energy that thrill gives her to get through the more routine and monotonous parts of her job. It buoys her up when her boss is unreasonable or her day is going badly. She thinks back to those moments and draws on the energy bank they have created.

Exercise 3 – Past influences

What you need: Your marked life history

Markers (hard copy) or symbols (computer)

A new file or notebook section

What you will do: Review each success to

identify how you achieved your successes

Why you will do this: To identify processes that lead to

your achievements

Part 1. How did I plan for this? What in my life prepared me for this experience?

Even the most serendipitous events in our lives can reveal some prior preparation. I won $10,000 on the $20,000 Pyramid while I was in graduate school. This looks like a totally serendipitous event, but that's not entirely true.

While attending the taping was in part luck, I had to project a positive image to get chosen for a try-out and I had to be sufficiently good at word association to get selected to be a contestant. Then, I had to be able to compete – without nervousness – on the air.

When I reviewed my own life history, I realized that I had spent years developing the skills that enabled me to win. I had years of experience in word association as a writer, as an English major, and in preparing for the SAT, the GRE, and the Miller's Analogy Test for school entrance. Almost every class in my Master's program had been videotaped. By the time I went to the taping, cameras meant nothing to me!

Connecting to the skills and experiences that have prepared you for a challenge helps you become clearer about what is at your disposal as you move to new challenges in the future. Marcia Sinetar author of *To Build the Life You Want, Create the Work You Love*, identified a group she calls

Creative Adapters; people who "don't simply adjust, they improvise with superior figuring-out skills." You are identifying your own skills in creative adaptation in this exercise.

Part 2.   *What did I do well?*

Sometimes, you are the last person to recognize your own strengths. This phenomenon is something I have seen often when working with organizations. People in organizations make extraordinary things happen every day but are often oblivious to their own success. "We got lucky," they say. "Somehow it just worked out." Don't believe this for a second! If you talk to these people long enough about how it "just happened," you can begin to tease out the thought, the skills, the prior practice that led to the right decisions at the right time.

You need to be able to do the analysis that tells you exactly why you succeeded every bit as much as organizations do. The problem in the workplace is that if the individuals that make up an organization are going to learn and grow – and repeat their successes – they have to understand what they did right. So do you. You have to understand the pattern of your successes. You need to know what you drew on from your prior experience at this moment so that next time you are faced with a challenge you can do the same thing.

How can you repeat a positive behavior if you don't know what it is? You aren't bragging here. You are connecting with your own strengths You are cutting through the underbrush that has grown over your path through life. You will need a clear view in both directions – behind you and up ahead – as you move towards your vision of the future. Machetes at the ready? Use the next two questions to help you cut through all those vines and branches.

Part 3: *What events in my past helped me understand this situation? What skills did I develop in other areas that I was able to transfer to this situation?*

Have you developed skills that you were able to rely on because you had this experience before, or did you generalize and transfer skills from other – seemingly unrelated - experiences? Are there events in your past that made you avoid certain options or choices? Did your past experience serve you well or did it prevent you from selecting the best plan of action as quickly as you might have wanted?

Ellen was an English teacher in a Middle School. She had been teaching for over ten years and had never considered doing anything else. When her daughter decided to get married and buy her first house within months of each other, Ellen was faced with a real financial challenge. As a teacher and single mother, she was making just about enough to get by. As a mother, of course she wanted to pay for the wedding – or at least a big chunk – and she wanted to help with the down payment on the house as well. So, when the opportunity to use her skills in a different way was offered to her, she decided to take it. She taught business writing to hospital personnel and did such a great job that she did repeat sessions straight through the summer and was able to not only help with the wedding and the house but have enough left over for a little splurge for herself!

For some of you, it may not seem like Ellen stretched much to make this transition, but in fact it took a lot of persuasion to get her to realize how easily her skills could be transferred. Once she moved from thinking of herself as teaching literature to realize how much time she spent teaching – and correcting grammar, she was on her way. Then, she was able to see how her skills as a family counselor and as a mentor to new teachers added experience in helping adults learn. Now she has a new skill set that she can use to generate additional income when she needs it.

Exercise 4 – Identify challenges

What you need: Your life history

Markers (hard copy) or symbols (computer)

A new file or notebook section

What you will do: Identify all the rough spots in your life

Why you will do   To learn how you have handled
this: challenges

Now let's look at the darker moments in your life history – the times when you were certain that there was nothing you could do to make life any better. We've all had our downward spirals. Go back and mark these sections in your life history. As you did in identifying your successes, select a new marker or pen for a handwritten document or a new symbol for a computer file. If you are working on the computer, if you haven't done so already, now would be a good time to create a key for yourself so that you can remember what all these symbols represent. After you have marked the appropriate sections in your life history, use a separate file or notebook section to answer the following questions:

Part 1. How was I feeling about this experience?

Some people see hardships or problems as challenges or opportunities. Others see them as insurmountable obstacles. Roberta has had surgery three times to remove growths, a challenge that she categorizes as a nuisance. Some of us would be making out our wills, sure that we are about to die of some terrible form of cancer? Why doesn't Roberta feel this way?

Roberta says that her body has a hobby of its own. It likes to grow things. Each time something new crops up, she is sure that it's just her body trying to annoy her with its little hobby. Although she takes each occurrence seriously, has all the tests, schedules the surgery, her recovery is never hampered by doom and gloom. Her attitude helps her take the surgery in stride. She says her current biggest concern is that eventually her breasts may look like patchwork quilts.

Leslie has had a series of medical problems and life changes that would cause most people to lie down in the middle of the road and just wait for a big truck to come along. She had been a college professor for years until a change eliminated her position. A serious car accident had left her in pain much of the time. It also gave her an intimate knowledge of traditional and non-traditional medicine.

Leslie decided to rethink her life and moved back to her family home, where she spent the next year caring for her dying mother. While she was still reeling from this experience – and trying to absorb what she now knew about senior care and treating terminal cancer, Leslie was diagnosed with a brain tumor. The tumor was successfully removed, but it left some residual deficits that made it pretty certain that Leslie would not be able to go back to college teaching, so she began to take stock of her skills.

By this time, Leslie was extremely knowledgeable about all kinds of health issues. She had always been interested in herbal remedies, nutrition and holistic treatment options. She also had originally been a business major and knew something about marketing. She had met just about every alternative practitioner in her area. She turned her career exploration to finding new ways to combine all these things and is now doing marketing for a naturalistic healer and volunteering at her local public radio station with an eye to having her own call-in show on health-related issues and resources.

Part 2. What was I imagining could happen? Were my worst fears realized?

There are two reasons for writing down your worst fears. One is that sometimes just seeing them in writing restores a sense of perspective. (No, forgetting to buy cat litter will not cause the end of civilization as we know it.) The second reason is that, for many people, this is a crucial step in remembering what planning was done to meet the challenge.

It may be that at the time you actually did engage in a little catastrophizing. Where did that lead? Were you paralyzed or did you move on? Sometimes, dealing with worst case scenarios helps spur creativity and leads to new – unexpected – courses of action.

Part 3. How was I feeling about myself during this experience? Did I feel in control or out of control?

We spoke earlier about identifying emotions. Sense of control is related to but may be slightly different than fear and anxiety, so it is important to look at it separately. Ruth began to sky dive precisely because the free fall portion of the jump felt to her like a complete loss of control. She felt that by becoming comfortable with not having control helped her learn to be more open and accepting of all the experiences life might bring her.

We see this same theme of letting go of control in Buddhism, in Gestalt therapy and in existentialism – the notion of living in the moment. How often have you done this? How comfortable were you?

Jaime has a high degree of comfort with chaos. Her life experience tells her that if she just lets go and enjoys the experience, chaos will settle into a positive outcome for her. This enables her to take risks with far less worry than most people. She plans and she work hard, but she feels that her confidence in a good outcome is what makes it all work.

Part 4.   What did I do to resolve the situation? What did I do for myself to cope?

Everyone reacts differently in what they perceive to be a crisis. Some have spent so much time creating contingency plans for every imaginable situation in life that they need only select the appropriate one and proceed. Others take the ostrich route, hide, do nothing, and wait for the crisis to blow over. A third group, true pessimists or fatalists (or both) to the end, simply remain passive, neither hiding nor taking action. They predict that the outcome will be bad and feel that nothing can be done to change it. They wait until the crisis has passed, shrug, and pick up the pieces – if there are any – and start over.

Then there are those whose lives seem to be one big crisis. One group is the perpetually problem-laden. Their lives never run smoothly, but they never see any of their problems as of their own making. They do have one special talent, however; they can always find someone to sort things out for them. People flock to these women's sides to solve their problems. Of course, these women also have a gift for making their helpers feel genuinely appreciative. They are grateful for all assistance and often reciprocate in every way that they can.

A second group mirrors the fatalists discussed earlier. They know that their lives will be a series of chaotic situations. They are not by nature planners, nor are they pessimists. They ride out every crisis, usually taking random actions without evaluating the impact of these actions. Sometimes everything works our wonderfully well; sometimes it's a bust. These women rarely know why.

A third group thrives on chaos. They expect that all change requires a certain amount of confusion and feel that life is a nugget of gold, shaped by fire and blows into something beautiful. Their confidence helps them get through crises.
Which type are you? Are you a whole other type? Does your crisis mode move you forward or hold you back?

Part 5. Who helped me? How? Did I ask for help or was it offered?

We rarely succeed in a vacuum, but we sometimes do not understand our own pattern for seeking help. Some women acknowledge the support of their friends at every turn; other may not realize just how much support they have had. This is a good place to do a quick inventory. You will be looking at two things at once. First, you will be creating a list of your supporters. This list will be organized into categories elsewhere, but as you create the list, you should begin to look for patterns. Do you rely on a wide circle of supporters or just a few? Do you rely on certain people for only one kind of help? Second, try to remember how you felt about actually asking for help. Some of us ask for help easily. Others have to be dangling off the edge of a cliff by one fingernail – and even then ... . Some enjoy assistance; others think it is often more trouble than it's worth.

Exercise 5 – Me and my emotions

What you need: Your marked life history
                  Markers (hard copy) or symbols
                  (computer)
                  A new file or notebook section
What you will do: Review each success to identify
                  the emotions related to the
                  experience
Why you will do To link your feelings to your
this: achievements

Now, let's look at how you were feeling at different points in your life. What you will be doing here is trying to look at the role emotion plays in your decision making pattern as well as the role emotion plays in your life. For some of us , there is a clear relationship between our emotional state and our behavior. For others, there is a stronger reliance on logic as a determiner of behavior and emotions play a stronger role. Some of us are drama queens. Some of us are very volatile; others keep a tight rein on our emotions.

Part 1.   When was I unhappy? Why? Are there specific themes of longings or lacks in my life? How did I resolve these feelings?

Of course, there is nothing wrong with being unhappy. Life will always be a mixture of pleasure and pain. Some of us take unhappiness in stride and move on; others get stuck in depression and can't seem to shake the darker moods. While sometimes you may be okay with an unhappy spell, other times you may want to do something to move beyond it. Looking at how you have reacted to sad times in the past may help you identify techniques you have used. You might also check for patterns of acceptance and avoidance. Do you take the good with the bad, acknowledge sadness or grief, work through it and move on or do you deny or avoid negative feelings?

Part 2.   When was I happiest? What did I do to contribute to my own happiness?

Doris is happiest when she is painting. Ruth reads. Jeannette walks for miles. Jane volunteers with a group that provides meals for people with AIDS. Carmen plays her guitar and sings Flamenco music. We can make our own happiness – usually by doing something productive. What energizes you?

Exercise 6 – Influences on my life

What you need: your marked life history
                   markers (hard copy) or symbols
                   (computer)
                   a new file or notebook section

What you will do: review each success to identify the
                   people who helped you along the way

Why you will do this: To remind yourself of who your friends are

Who influenced me? Who have I influenced? Who are all the people you have touched in your life? How did you influence them? We often think that we go through life unnoticed. We think that we have not contributed anything to the greater good. It is easy to fall into a depression and feel useless. This exercise will remind you of just how much of an influence you are. Make the list as long as you can.

As we move through our own life, we touch so many others lives, yet we rarely are aware of the impact we have on others. Use your life history as a resource for this list. Work with two columns here so that, as names occur to you (or descriptions if the names are gone) you can add them to either side. Some names may belong on both sides of the list.

Exercise 7 – Change patterns

What you need: your marked life history

markers (hard copy) or symbols (computer)

a new file or notebook section

What you will do: review each life change identify any

patterns in how you handle change

Why you will do this: To identify processes that you want

to repeat or change

What patterns did I notice? How do I react in action? Each of us handles life's challenges in our own unique way, but there are some general patterns that emerge when we look at different coping or problem solving strategies. See which category seems to best fit the information you've uncovered about your own behavior. If none of these sounds like you, create your own. You are not trying to fit into someone else's boxes here; you are trying to understand how you have operated in the past so that you can make clearer decisions about which behaviors you want to maintain or strengthen and which you want to give up or modify. Once you have actually named or labeled your coping strategy, it may be easier for you to understand this as a chosen set of behaviors rather than happenstance or dumb luck. Second, it may be worth considering varying your strategy. If you have used only one strategy and consider yourself to be unsuccessful, what else might you begin to try in the future?

Here are some change types:

Planners

have contingency plans for everything. They love to think ahead about what they might do in any situation and imagine that they are always ready for anything. Remember Michelle? Because she was in the habit of planning, when she was faced with the need to change her life to accommodate Leslie's illness she used the habit of planning to face the crisis calmly and rationally. In the face of emergency, planners stop and make a plan; they research, they consult others. They move slowly and deliberately, but they do move. They take their time, then take well-considered action.

Daredevils

leap into the fray and never look back. They have high confidence that everything will turn out fine. They trust others to bail them out if necessary. They may have no idea who that somebody will be; they just move through life sure that something will happen and everything will work out. They are the eternal optimists of change. Some of them are always in scrapes of some sort. They may have brilliant successes or dismal failures. In either case, they will still be ready for that next leap.

Chaos Creatures

feel that in life most change arises out of chaos. They have great faith in their ability to thrive on chaos and come through it better and stronger than ever. They excel at on-the-spot planning, have good research skills and can juggle multiple priorities. Multi-tasking is not just a computer term for these people – they usually have two or three projects going on at once and a couple more on the back burner. A chaos creature is an excellent synthesizer – always looking for patterns and seeing possibilities. They love to hypothesize based on very little information.

Waiters

just hold still until everything is over. If disaster strikes, they wait calmly, then sort through the debris and rebuild if necessary. If life brings them fame and fortune, they wait till the cheering dies down and then figure out how to make the best use of all this good stuff. They are not prone to take action at the front end of change; rather, they let change roll over them, then make the best possible use of whatever happens. They may be calculating the odds during the change or they may remain passive until everything settles down a bit. Like the chaos creatures, they are excellent synthesizers;

unlike them, they operate best from a position of calm and in possession of all the facts.

Which type are you? How can you use this information to help you handle future changes? Does your style make you more effective or get in your way? We discussed varying your style. Sometimes, waiting makes sense, and you should go with your natural inclination, but sometimes a waiter will wait too long and action will no longer be possible. On the other hand, daredevils may plunge in headlong and end up going over a cliff.

Knowing what your personal patterns are provides a framework for career choices. Use the space below to summarize your patterns so that you can refer to them as you move on to career choices.

Vision, Goals and Legacy Blueprint Playbook

A step-by-step guide to creating a vision for your ideal life and getting out of your own way

Vision Blueprint

Preparing to Write Your Vision Statement

The vision that you glorify in your mind, the ideal that you enthrone in your heart, this you will build your life by, and this you will become.
Anonymous

How Will You be Remembered? Writing Your Eulogy

As you create your Vision Blueprint, it's helpful to begin with the long view. You would view the terrain before beginning to plan a house. How will you want the house situated? Where are the best views? Are there natural features that you will want to take advantage of? So too you may want to look at the overall shape of your life.

One way to begin to see what's important in your life is to look ahead to the end of your years. To do this, you are about to write your own eulogy. This may sound morbid, but it really isn't. The purpose of this exercise is to craft a personal vision.

Organizations do this all the time. They hire expensive consultants to lead them in future searches or "blue skying" because they know that they can't grow or change unless they know where they want to be – the organizational vision. Just as for organizations, as an individual, when you understand that vision– what you hope to achieve during the course of your life – your life goals will become clear to you.

If you find the idea of writing a eulogy upsetting or threatening, picture yourself writing a testimonial being given about you at a big awards banquet honoring your lifetime achievements.

Find a quiet, private space and something to write on. Turn off the television. Get rid of any distractions. Take a few deep breaths. Clear your mind of other concerns. If you wish, close your eyes.

Imagine a room full of people who love you who have come together to celebrate your life. Imagine that you have accomplished everything that you ever hoped to do. Your every dream has been fulfilled. Everyone who is important to you is gathered to talk about the wonderful person you were and about your many accomplishments. If you listen, you can hear the speakers. Write down what they are saying about you.

What are all the things you have accomplished? Have you traveled? Where? What have you created? Have your written or painted or played the flute or knitted or gardened? Did you cook for friends? Volunteer at a soup kitchen? Teach someone something? Send perfect postcards or birthday cards?

A vision is not just a picture of what could be; it is an appeal to our better selves, a call to become something more.
Rosabeth Moss Kanter

What skills have you shared with the people assembled? Who are the people who remember you? What do they remember you for? What kind of friend were you? What did they say about your character – about who you are as a person?

Write as quickly as you can and don't censor your writing. When you have written as much as you can, put it aside overnight. Now go back to your eulogy and read it very slowly. What did you leave out? Make any additions you feel are important.

1. Identify Goals

Go back over your eulogy and highlight your accomplishments, then create a separate list of these accomplishments. What will you need to do to make all of the things that you heard a reality? Those accomplishments you have yet to achieve represent potential goals. They will serve as the basis for planning your life goals.

2. Identify Values

Go back one more time and highlight the things people said about you. Look at these in relation to your accomplishments and generate a list of things that you value or that represent your values (e.g. family ties, hard work, friendship).

Developing a Personal Vision and Mission Statement

Vision Statement

Your personal vision statement should describe what you ultimately envision the greater purpose of your life to be, in terms of growth, values, contributions to society, etc. Self-reflection is a vital activity if you want to develop a meaningful vision. Once you have defined your vision, you can begin to develop strategies for moving toward that vision. Part of this includes the development of a mission statement.

What do you want for the rest of your life? Take a few minutes to write down your personal vision. This will be based on your goals and values.

Sample Personal Vision Statements

To create a foundation for women who need help getting beyond childhood abuse and neglect.

To reach audiences worldwide with my writing and speaking.

Sample Corporate Vision Statements

To be the company that best understands and satisfies the product, service and self-fulfillment needs of women - globally.

"To bring inspiration and innovation to every athlete*in the world"* If you have a body, you are an athlete.

Our vision is every book ever printed in any language all available in 60 seconds.

Mission Statement

Vision statements and mission statements are very different. Your mission statement is the vision translated into written form. It is a concrete expression of how you will bring your vision to life. A mission statement should be a short and concise statement of goals and priorities.

Your mission statement should be a concise statement of strategy, and it should fit with your vision. The mission should answer three questions:

1. What will I do?
2. How will I do it?
3. For whom will I do it?

What will I do? This question should be answered in terms of what are the concrete and psychological needs that you want to fulfill.

How will I do it? This question captures the more technical elements.

For whom will I do it? The answer to this question is also vital, as it will help you focus your efforts.

Legacy Questions

These may help you clarify your vision and mission.

1. Is it important to me to give something back to my community or the world?

2. Do I want to ensure that others inherit money and/or material things from me?

3. Do I want to leave something behind that creates memories for others?

4. How do I want to be remembered?

5. What am I doing to create a legacy?

6. In what ways do I want to influence other people?

7. Are there causes in which I want to become involved?

8. Are there skills that I would like to teach to others?

Goals Blueprint

A step-by-step guide to creating goals for your ideal life

Goals: Why Bother?

"Would you tell me, please, which way I ought to go from here?"
"That depends a good deal on where you want to get to," said the Cat.
"I don't much care where—" said Alice.
"Then it doesn't matter which way you go," said the Cat.
Lewis Carroll
Alice's Adventures in Wonderland

Many people I've spoken with in the past year say that they don't plan – they just let their lives emerge. Initially, this might sound good. Then, after a few questions, it becomes clear that this may not be the best action plan. They fall into jobs that pretty much work. They fall into relationships that are okay. They hope that something good will happen – and sometimes it does. They like to attribute outcomes to luck.

If this is you, stop reading right now. You don't need to learn how to set goals. You're not really interested in changing your life, and that's okay. It will simply be a waste of time for you to read this book.

If, however, you think that your life could be different in some way, please keep reading, do the exercises, and try not to chortle all the time as your life keeps holding less and less of what you don't want and more and more of what you truly desire.

Why set goals? The process helps you dream bigger dreams or simply clarify exactly what you want. Goal setting provides you with a big vision, a clear action plan, and specific techniques for overcoming any obstacles that might block you from getting what you really want.

Creating a Blueprint

Have you ever watched people looking at a blueprint? Done it yourself? It always looks like such a wonderful experience – pouring over the details, moving from the large view to the most minute details and back again.

In the past, I've written about goal mapping, and now I'm shifting my language around goals. Why? A map will show you how to get from one place to another, and that's a good thing, but it strikes me that a blueprint could be even better. A blueprint shows you what the endpoint will look like – the shape, size, and relative position of each room. A blueprint can be readjusted. It's both personal and tangible. It situates your goal within the rest of your life rather than simply giving you directions to reach a destination.

Begin with a Vision

> *People only see what they are prepared to see.*
> Ralph Waldo Emerson

> *Vision is the art of seeing things invisible.*
> Jonathan Swift

Any GPS or mapping device will ask you a few questions about your journey – Where are you now? Where are you going? How are you traveling (walking, taking public transportation, driving)? Do you want the fast route or the scenic one? It won't ask you abut your vision of how the trip will unfold.

If you were speaking with an architect, your initial conversation would be all about your vision. It would focus on how you will live in the space you are creating. This vision would inform specific questions involved about your blueprint. How big will this structure be? Each room? How many rooms do you want? How do the rooms interrelate?

Outlining the Structure

Let's get started by concentrating on the overall structure. Go back to the previous section. What's your vision? How do you see yourself at the end of the process? What does your completed structure look like? What is the general outline of your blueprint?

My Vision

_____

_____

_____

_____

_____

_____

What do you see as the overall size and shape of whatever you are building? This is generally called an overarching goal. It's an end point. Think of this overarching goal as your mental picture of your completed building (project). How big is it? How many stories? Why is it there? How will you use it? Write down the biggest goal you can think of – a real stretch goal – something that will definitely expand your comfort zone.

My Overarching Goal

_____

_____

_____

_____

_____

_____

Now you have a goal – an outline for your blueprint. Your architect is going to want to start getting details, though. Perhaps the simplest way to bring your goal from general to specific is to use a proven goal-setting formula: S-M-A-R-T goals.

S-M-A-R-T Goals

Check your goal against the S-M-A-R-T criteria and tweak away until it's as clear and strong as possible. If you don't have a really good sense of what the completed building looks like, it will be hard to plan the individual rooms. The criteria are described below.

S - Specific

All my life, I always wanted to be somebody. Now I see that I should have been more specific.
Lily Tomlin

Have you been as specific as possible? Can you clearly picture this structure? Is this a ranch house, a beach shack, a chateau in Switzerland? Perhaps you want to create the perfect apartment in Manhattan with views of a park and of water, complete concierge services, three bedrooms, an office, a library, a formal dining room, a breakfast nook, a laundry room, a balcony area large enough to entertain at least six people, three and a half bathrooms, and a state-of-the-art kitchen, within four blocks of major public transportation. That's pretty specific. As a business goal, you might say: Within the next 24 months, I want to build a coaching and consulting business working with high-potential, high-performing, affluent women who want to put in the time and energy to create their ideal lives and/or businesses, and I want to have a consistent income of $1 million from direct services and $1 million from passive income while working no more than 20 hours per week, no more than 30 weeks per year.

My Overarching Goal Made Specific

_____

_____

_____

_____

_____

_____

M - Measurable

Measure what is measurable and make measurable what is not so.
Galileo Galilei

Can you build actual, measurable criteria into your goal? The examples above have measures – number of rooms, type of rooms, dollar figures for earnings, time figures for how much work, standards for clients.

My Overarching Goal Made Measurable

_____

_____

_____

_____

_____

_____

A - Achievable

Is this something you can actually do? Don't get into all the details here – you'll be developing subgoals and action plans later. Is this something that you feel comfortable creating an action plan around? Is this a blueprint for something you can build?

My Overarching Goal Made Achievable

_____

_____

_____

_____

_____

_____

R - Realistic

To be realistic today is to be visionary. To be realistic is to be starry-eyed.
Hubert Humphrey

Can this actually happen? Can you find examples of what you want to build? I've been in apartments very similar to the one I've described; I know entrepreneurs who have the business I've described. I know that these are things that can – and do – exist.

My Overarching Goal Made Realistic

_____

_____

_____

_____

_____

_____

T - Timely and Time-Framed

Is this the right time for me to work on this goal? Do I have a realistic idea of how long it will take? If you've been paying careful attention to the examples, you'll notice that the first example is not time-framed, although it may be timely. Supporting goals – rooms on the blueprint – will need to be created before a time frame can be determined for this goal. The second example, though, is both timely and time-framed. This is driven by desire and research. Supporting goals will all have time frames, so it will be possible to see how quickly this can be built.

My Overarching Goal Made Time-Framed

_____

_____

_____

_____

_____

_____

Planning the Rooms: Developing Subgoals

Always design a thing by considering it in its next larger context – a chair in a room, a room in a house, a house in an environment, an environment in a city plan.
Eliel Saarinen

The design of good houses requires an understanding of both the construction materials and the behavior of real humans.
Peter Morville

Planning is bringing the future into the present so that you can do something about it now.
Alan Lakein

Congratulations! You now have the overall shape of your structure (goal) and can begin to complete your blueprint. Next, we'll flesh out your subgoals – the number of rooms on your blueprint.

You have created the outline of your blueprint for your ideal future. You have a big, overarching goal. You know what this structure will look like – at least from the outside – in a very specific way. But a blueprint is more than a shell. It provides exact specifications for each room. In the same way, your overarching goal is made up of a number of smaller goals.

Let's get some rooms on that blueprint! Just as you don't jump from an empty shell to a fully completed house, you don't jump from wherever you are today to a fully realized overarching goal. Just as your house will have clearly defined rooms, your goal blueprint will have clearly defined subgoals.

This is the business goal from Part 1:

Within the next 24 months, I want to build a coaching and consulting business working with high-potential, high-performing, affluent women who want to put in the time and energy to create their ideal lives and/or businesses and I want to have a consistent income of $1 million from direct services and $1 million from passive income while working no more than 20 hours per week, no more than 30 weeks per year.

Subgoals might include:

1. Identify ways to get in front of my ideal clients.
2. Develop persuasive reasons for these women to select my services.
3. Create materials for live and self-paced coaching programs.
4. Create an effective sign-up and distribution system.

Each of these represents a room on the blueprint. The next step is to see how these rooms will best fit together. What's the optimal flow through the space? What size will each room be? How does each relate to the others? This is accomplished by organizing and fleshing out the subgoals. When you enter a house, does it make sense to come into a bedroom? Probably not. But could the kitchen or an office take as much space as the living room? Could be. The rooms on your blueprint need to be organized in a way that is logical for you. So, too, your subgoals should flow in a way that is logical for you.

Organizing is what you do before you do something, so that when you do it, it is not all mixed up.
A. A. Milne

The goals above might work well in the order they were initially presented. But there are other configurations that work well.

1. Develop persuasive reasons for these women to select my services.
2. Identify ways to get in front of my ideal clients.
3. Create an effective sign-up and distribution system
4. Create materials for live and self-paced coaching programs.

It might make more sense to have systems in place before taking action.

Rearrange your subgoals until you have a flow that works for you. Then, define the purpose of each room. Be very explicit. Develop and clarify each goal using the S-M-A-R-T model.

Identifying Obstacles and Creating Action Plans

A good architect understands that each project may have what appears to be limitations. A good blueprint helps uncover those potential limitations or obstacles so that the architect and client can figure out how to address these real or perceived obstacles. Doesn't it make sense, then, that you might want to look at potential obstacles to reaching your goals? If you can identify potential obstacles, then you can develop a plan to overcome them.

Obstacles don't have to stop you. If you run into a wall, don't turn around and give up. Figure out how to climb it, go through it, or work around it.
Michael Jordan

Whether we're prepared or not, life has a habit of thrusting situations upon us.
Lucille Ball

This is subgoal #4:

Create materials for live and self-paced coaching programs.

Rewritten as a S-M-A-R-T goal, it would look like this:

Within the next six months, repurpose, recombine, and expand current articles, exercises, and workshop materials to create one cohesive two-day workshop, one two-hour promotional workshop, one six-part teleclass, and two four-part e-courses.

What are some obstacles to achieving this goal? What action planning is necessary to overcome each obstacle?

Obstacle 1: There might be time limitations.

Action plan?

Review schedule and create a number of short periods of time to devote to writing.
-OR-
Outsource the rewrites.

Obstacle 2: There might not be enough material.

Action plan?

Have guest authors contribute.
-OR-
Research additional material.
-OR-
Hire a researcher.
-OR-
Pilot the material and add contributions from the ensuing discussions.
-OR-
Use questionnaires or focus groups to generate content.

Get the idea? When you look at your blueprint from the broadest perspective, hone in to understand the general interior, and then focus narrowly on the exact contents of each room, you will have the building of your dreams. Your goal blueprint provides you with the big picture and with the specific details you will want in order to create the life of your dreams.

I don't think of myself as a poor deprived ghetto girl who made good. I think of myself as somebody who from an early age knew I was responsible for myself, and I had to make good.
Oprah Winfrey

Remember, success is not measured by heights attained but by obstacles overcome. We're going to pass through many obstacles in our lives: good days, bad days. But the successful person will overcome those obstacles and constantly move forward.
Bruce Jenner

Success is not the key to happiness. Happiness is the key to success. If you love what you are doing, you will be successful.

Albert Schweitzer

Clearing Conflicting Intentions

Are You Getting in Your Own Way?

What's Holding You Back?

How often do you feel like that mythical beast from Dr. Doolittle – the PushmePullyou? You really want to take that next step to move forward in some part of your life only to find that it's as if your feet are stuck in the mud. You want something, but part of you wants something else that may even be the complete opposite. So you go nowhere.

People usually take steps to meet their desires or carry out their intentions unless there is some internal force or energy that is holding them back. We call this conflicting desires or conflicting intentions. It's like having two energy forces pulling you in two different directions. You are stuck in the middle of this tug-of-war and it's probably making you very, very tired.

When we know what we want and work towards that goal, life goes along pretty smoothly, but when we run into barriers, we need to stop and do some work.

The barriers that stop us in our tracks are self-imposed, so we need strategies to break through those artificial walls and get what we want. You may think that your barriers are outside yourself, but, really, they are in your own mind – in your attitude and in the reasons you tell yourself you can't have what you want. As Henry Ford said, Whether you think you can or you can't, you're right!

So, this whole process of moving forward begins with clearing the self-imposed barriers in our lives that keep us from moving forward.

Wake-up Call

The first step is a wake-up call. This is that little aha moment when you realize that you aren't getting the results you want. You begin to realize that something is holding you back.

What's something you've said you want to do but are not actually doing?

What's Stopping You?

Most of us carry out their intentions unless there is some underlying issue that conflicts with our stated desire. If we look at the physics underlying attraction, we understand that EVERYTHING is made up of energy. This includes thoughts, actions, intentions, things and circumstances. They are all made up of energy. So, our desires have energy which causes things to happen or come to us. We still need to take action to make things happen, but even when this involves hard work, it isn't a continuous struggle. However, when things DON'T happen, there is almost always an unseen or unspoken intention that has more energy than our desire. These conflicting intentions represent mixed messages we give ourselves and often come from old messages from our past that we are carrying forward.

Here's an example: A writer felt that achieving best-seller status would mean she would stop working and sit around eating chocolates. She's an award-winning poet and still working hard. The image she's holding is of what her parents have done, not how she has chosen to lead her life, but still, the conflict between wanting success and fearing success will ruin her life holds her back.

Reality Check

People act differently on intentions based on how important the intention is to them. Do a quick check to be sure that this intention is important to you. Is it a distraction? What do you REALLY want to do?

You mentioned that you want to work on _____. What have you done so far? Has that been hard or easy? What are you NOT doing?

How have you tried to get going? Is that working for you? Why not?

Clearing Conflicting Thoughts

Everything that happens is a collaboration between you and the universe.

Intentions are energy.

All of our intentions are prone to being sabotaged by conflicting intentions, especially the intentions that are really meaningful to us.

Restate your intention. Then outline, in no ore than five steps, how you plan to achieve that intention. Are you acting on this plan or stuck?

Sit with your plan for a while. Examine each step by asking the following questions:
What's really going on here?
What story am I telling myself?
Is that true?
What evidence do I have to support that?

If you find evidence to support your story, perhaps this is the wrong intention, or perhaps the story is based on faulty interpretations. Now ask:
Where does my story come from?
What might be a reframe or an alternate explanation?

Moving Forward

We get conflicting intentions from our past conditioning and socialization. Stories that protected us in the past might no longer serve us.

When you have an intention, whether it's to get a close parking space (in the moment, it's easy, it happens or it doesn't but there's little or no baggage) or get 10 new clients (longer term, future-oriented,) the next thing you want to do is be very aware of the conflicts.

You want your conflicting intentions to come to the surface. Then you can do something about them. You want to design an environment that causes your conflicting intentions to come to the surface. This is the thing they never teach you about in an affirmations class!

Nurturing Blueprint

Playbook

A step-by-step guide to adding nurturing to your ideal life

Nurturing

Webster's Dictionary defines "nurturing" as furthering the development of another. For the development of a blueprint for this aspect of your life, you'll be looking at the broader issue of nurturing, rather than focusing more narrowly on parenting, because there are so many options open to us at different stages of life.

Earlier in life, you may be concerned with issues around having children. Later, you may be involved with aging parents as well as children leaving home, postponing leaving, or even returning home. Some of you will be raising your grandchildren. Some of you have given birth; some have adopted; some have been wonderful aunts, mentors, teachers, and friends. Some have rescued and nurtured animals. Some have grown magnificent gardens. All of these represent a form of nurturing.

Let's begin the Nurturing Blueprint by examining the overall shape of your structure. What is your current family situation? Who and/or what do you nurture?

_____

_____

_____

_____

_____

_____

_____

_____

_____

Crossroads: Decision Points in Adulthood

Throughout life, there are several points where you may be making decisions about what nurturing looks like for you.

Early to Mid-adulthood

From their twenties through early to mid forties, most women have a variety of concerns about career and family, including when – or whether – to have children, whether to parent as a single or part of a couple, and levels of involvement in parenting for partner and other family members and/or friends. These are decision crossroads that I've called Which Way Should I Go? Family or Career? Career or Family? How Do I Do It All?

Middle Adulthood

These crossroads overlap with the next cluster, which includes Career or Family? How Can I Do it All? And, sometimes, Is That All There Is?

These phases of life include decisions about having or raising children, balancing family and career, and participating in nurturing someone else's children or aging relatives.

Women at these crossroads are often master jugglers. Those who have decided to have children may have concerns ranging from selecting a preschool to sending the last child off into the world. They may be concerned with paying for daycare and college at the same time. Some are also providing an increased level of care for their own parents, and some may be dealing with health issues of their own and contemplating retirement or second careers.

Mature Adulthood

Women at the next set of crossroads may also be concerned with all of the same issues as their sisters at the previous crossroads. Some women are giving birth or adopting late in life. Some who have remained childless – by choice or circumstance – may find themselves involved later in life in relationships with a significant other who has children or grandchildren. Some may be enjoying the so-called empty nest, while others may be mourning the loss of nurturing possibilities. Whatever the situation, women can find many creative adaptations to meet their need to nurture. These crossroads are Is That All There Is? What Do I Need for the Rest of the Journey? Serenity or Longing? Sometimes, it might be hard to realize how many options are available or how to adapt to starting over in relation to nurturing.

Where do you see yourself on this continuum?

_____

_____

_____

_____

_____

Now that you have a general outline for your building, let's get some idea of how many rooms you might want. If you are growing your family, you may want more space than if you are shedding responsibilities and relationships.

How important is nurturing to you? Some people want to nurture in as many ways as possible, while for others, one person or one pet or a small garden may be sufficient.

What would your ideal nurturing situation be? Be specific about who you would ideally nurture and about the number of people or things you want to nurture.

114

Child-Free by Choice and Empty Nest: Loss or Opportunity?

According to Tori DeAngelis, writing for the National Association of Social Workers,

> The so-called "empty nest syndrome," which describes the depression that supposedly arises when one's children leave home, is far from inevitable. More often than not, the positives of this period of life outweigh the negatives . . . . Studies show that women in their early 50s often feel satisfaction that they've successfully raised and launched their children, a new sense of freedom and well-being, and a desire to tap latent talents and abilities. . . . That said, women's work histories are often erratic because of parenting and caretaking duties. Many women leave work for periods of time, work part-time or take low-paying jobs, for instance.

Kathryn Griffin, in her essay on not having children, asks

if I don't have children, who will be there for me as I grow older? I think about the traditional transitions of a woman's life as she shifts from single woman to wife to mother to grandmother, and I wonder what milestones will mark the years of my life. Who will pore over the traces of my days, searching for meaning and a sense of connection? In a world where ancestors are universal, what will it mean to be a woman without descendants?

Griffin goes on to point out:

Even in coping with the losses and difficulties of old age, childless women do just as well as mothers. True, the social networks of the childless tend to be smaller, because they have neither children nor grandchildren, but they do not

117

report feeling more lonely and isolated than parents.

Anthropologist Robert L. Rubinstein of the Philadelphia Geriatric Center studied 90 childless women over 60 and found that although some women did express regret at their childless state, they found value and meaning in life and came up with satisfying alternatives for whatever nurturing urges they had, including strong connections with younger people: nieces and nephews, fellow church members, or longtime neighbors.

Sociologists Ingrid Connidis and Julie McMullin of the University of Western Ontario studied nearly 700 Canadian men and women over age 55 and found that those who chose childlessness were just as happy as parents who had good relationships with their children. And they were happier than those parents who described their relationships with their children as distant.

This picture of happy, well-functioning, child-free women is obscured by society's discomfort with women who do not fit classic role stereotypes. Women who don't have children, psychologist Mardy Ireland says, are assumed to be either career-crazed imitation men or sad, barren spinster types. Neither stereotype acknowledges that women can have rich and balanced lives without children of their own.

There are many ways to build a family and many ways to nurture. Hospitals and custodial facilities are full of children to cuddle or play with. Animal rescue groups always need foster care for pets awaiting adoption – and thousands of pets are looking for good homes. Community gardens need tending. Big Brothers, Big Sisters and other mentoring groups are eager or volunteers. Elders, people in need of long-term care, recent arrivals to the country or to your neighborhood, and children in daycare or after-school programs can all benefit from whatever time you can spare to nurture them. Or perhaps nurturing yourself is sufficient for you.

What opportunities to nurture are available to you?

_____

_____

_____

_____

_____

_____

_____

Unexpected Nurturing: Grandparents as Parents and Eldercare

At midlife, some women are still caring for children – especially women who postponed childbirth. Some are having their first grandchildren and spending increasing amounts of time caring for parents or other aging relatives. Others may unexpectedly find themselves caring for their children's children.

Earlier in life, our parents provided backup, support, counsel, and sometimes even financial assistance, but now we may be providing all these things to them while we are still providing for our children. Some women may find themselves not just part of a generational sandwich but part of a club sandwich, with aging parents, minor or boomerang children, and the added responsibility of grandchildren.

According to Deb Gebeke, family science specialist, in 1996, the American Association of

Retired Persons reported a 17 percent jump in the number of children cared for in grandparent-only households in one year – 1992 to 1993. This is contrasted with a gradual 6 percent rise over the prior 22 years. The Census Bureau figures that 3.4 million children are raised by grandparents or other relatives. And, 44 percent of the nation's grandparents spend 100 or more hours a year taking care of grandkids.

For most grandparents, grandchildren are meant to be enjoyed, then returned. Resuming the role of primary caretaker can be a big adjustment in terms of loss of free time, strain on limited resources, and finding ways to work around physical limitations. There also may be deep psychological issues to deal with, as the grandchildren may have come from unstable households or may be traumatized by the loss of their parents.

Of the various legal arrangements that exist, according to Dana Wilson of the Child Welfare

League of America, kinship care is becoming the "preferred option" to keep children within their own families. California, Minnesota, New Jersey, Maryland, and other states have passed or are considering laws incorporating kinship care into foster-care networks. In New York City alone, the children in kinship foster care rose from 45 in 1986 to 23,600 in 1991. In private kinship care, custody remains with a family member. Relative caregivers are not eligible for child-care payments, although other assistance may be available. Private kinship care arrangements take various forms:

- The grandparent is caretaker, but the parent retains legal custody and can make any decisions regarding the kids.

- The grandparent has temporary legal custody, which public housing and some school districts require of caregivers. Legal custodians make decisions concerning daily care of the child, but parents are still involved in major decisions.

- The grandparent adopts the child, and rights of the birth parents are terminated.

Divorce is another situation that may alter the role grandparents play. The following guidelines for dealing with grandchildren after divorce are from http://www.ext.colostate.edu/pubs/consumer/10241.html:

- When a couple divorces, a natural tendency of grandparents is to side with their child against his or her spouse. The suggested guideline, however, is to remain (at least outwardly) neutral. It is in the grandchild's best interest to keep matters as amicable as possible.
- Do not attempt to get grandchildren to take sides in their parents' divorce. Sometimes, one or both of the divorcing parents will attempt to use grandparents as a weapon in the struggle for a grandchild's loyalty. These attempts should be resisted, and dealt with in an open manner.
- Stay flexible. If a recently divorced in-law feels that weekly visits by the former spouse's parents are too difficult to manage for the

moment, the grandparents should, in most instances, not argue. They should settle for a different – even if less frequent – schedule. Generally, patience will most likely pay off in a better relationship.

Dealing with Aging Parents

According to Vanderbilt University, as more and more adult children face caring for their aging parents in the coming decades, an expert on the clinical psychology of aging says the key to dealing with these types of situations is to discuss them before they become a reality.

By 2050, more than 20 percent of Americans will be over age 65 and living longer, healthier lives than ever before, according to Dr. Brian D. Carpenter, of Washington University, St. Louis. And the inevitable help they will need in their advanced years will fall mostly on the shoulders of their adult children.

Planning and good family communications can help the "sandwich generation" work through the challenges of caring for aging parents while dealing with their own issues of child-rearing, housing, finances, work, and middle-age health, says Dr. Carpenter, the principal investigator of a research project examining family support networks.

Dr. Carpenter goes on to offer the following advice:

- Don't put off talking about caregiving issues.
- Take small bites – but not of each other. You don't have to sit down and have a whole weekend where you'll map out every possible health care situation and preference. Schedule a conversation and give yourself enough time to do it in small chunks over a long period of time.
- Take responsibility. Don't assume that your parent, sister, or child is going to bring it up. Everybody in the family needs to take some responsibility for having the conversations.

- Flex and forgive. Be flexible and be willing to think about ways you can forgive one another for things that may have happened in the past that may be getting in the way of having good family relationships in the future.

He points out that many families find it difficult to have frank discussions about what support is expected and what support can actually be given. People may get upset and feelings may get hurt, but better that than people feeling angry, hostile, and upset without ever airing their feelings. Some families may find it helpful to bring in an objective mediator, such as a social worker, lawyer, physician, or psychologist, to help sort out these issues. In fact, a new career of "certified family life educators" has emerged to help families deal with such topics.

As Paula J. Wart points out, caretakers need care, too! In an article for Vanderbilt University, she says:

Nearly one in four American families provide some level of care to friends and relatives who have health problems or disabilities and need help. Recent surveys found that more than seven million people are informal caregivers to older adults. Another 26 million caregivers provide care to adult family members with disabilities or chronic illnesses.

Caregiving can be emotionally, socially, and financially draining. Wart describes the signs of strain as identified by the Alzheimer's Association:

- Anger
- Anxiety
- Denial
- Depression
- Exhaustion
- Health problems
- Irritability

- Lack of concentration
- Social withdrawal

If you are caught in a nurturing sandwich, you will want to work hard to make time to nurture yourself. Caring for a person with Alzheimer's disease or other kinds of dementia can be overwhelming. But so can caring for someone with a terminal illness or an activity-limiting disability or trying to keep up with the grandchildren. Any type of caregiving can be unbearable without support from family, friends, and community resources.

The following suggestions are provided by Vanderbilt University:

- Find out everything you can about your loved one's condition, and educate yourself on recommended caregiving techniques.
- Be realistic about what you can do, and realize your limitations.
- Eat a healthy diet rich in fruits, vegetables and whole grains and low in saturated fat.

129

Ask your health care provider about taking a multivitamin as well.

- Try to get enough sleep and rest.
- Find time for some exercise most days of the week. Regular exercise can help reduce stress and improve your health in many ways.
- Learn relaxation techniques to help manage stress.
- See your health care provider for a checkup. Talk to your provider about symptoms of illness or depression that you may be having.
- Get counseling if needed if you experience symptoms of anxiety or depression.
- Stay in touch with friends. Social activities can help keep you feeling connected and help with stress. Faith-based groups can offer support and help to caregivers.
- Find a support group for other caregivers in your situation (such as caring for a person with dementia). Many support groups are available online through the Internet.
- Accept help when it is offered, and get help when you need it. It may not be easy to ask

for help, and you may need to make very specific requests. But getting help from family and friends will benefit you and the person you are caring for.

- Arrange for one or two days of respite care for the care receiver, either at home or in an assisted living facility.

- Help your loved one function as independently as possible. Look into assist equipment, such as walkers and raised toilet seats. In one study, care receivers who used assist devices required four fewer hours of care per week than those who didn't use them.

- Keep alert for any excuse to laugh. Focusing on the good things you're doing can go a long way toward giving you a positive mental outlook.

Finally, seek assistance. One resource is **www.eldercare.gov**

How will you nurture yourself?

_____

_____

_____

_____

_____

_____

_____

_____

Nurturing Blueprint – Questions

How will I create a space for nurturing in my life?

How can I deal with parenting or assisting my own parents, if necessary?

How will I deal with my children growing up?

How do I feel about my children leaving home?

What will I do if faced with the unexpected return of my children?

Can I meet my nurturing needs through my pets?

Can I meet my nurturing needs through mentoring?

Will I want to nurture by volunteering or being of service to others?

How do I feel about my adult children returning home?

How will I feel about being in the position of parenting my grandchildren or the children of other family members?

How do I feel about my children having left home?

How do I want to relate to grandchildren, if I have them?

How will I relate to my partner or spouse's children from prior relationships?

How will I create a family of choice or support network?

How will I continue to create space for nurturing in my life?

Relationships

Blueprint

Playbook

Relationships

One thing that remains consistent as we move through life is our need to be connected to others. Our relationship networks may change as we age, move into and perhaps out of relationships, gain and lose friendships, or find that the demands of our lives change the number of connections we can maintain.

Relationships are such an integral part of our lives that it's a surprise that so many of us don't pay close attention to them. Your relationship Blueprint will help you examine the current status of your relationships and your relationship needs. This is a Blueprint that you're likely to want to go back to on a regular basis. Relationship needs change over lie. Our ability to make new friends changes. What we want out of relationships changes. And, as we age, loss factors into the status of our relationships.

'Cause at the end of the day, honestly,

at the end of the day when you're in your death bed and that's it, I think it's the relationships you've had and the people that you've touched and the people that have touched you that matter.

Julie Benz

Cherish your human connections - your relationships with friends and family.
Barbara Bush

Who are your three most important relationships with? Why is each important?

_____

_____

_____

_____

Friends

In her essay, *The healing power of female friendships*, Kathy English reminds us that new studies are providing strong evidence that female friendships are vital to a woman's health and may well prolong her life. She goes on to say:

Certainly, women seem driven to form friendships with other females. Right from our early days in play groups and pre-school, little girls are drawn to one another and grow up to develop more intimate friendships than boys do and also create larger social networks. Women have long gathered in groups to support one another and share their interests. In the pioneer days, we held quilting bees. These days we gather and gab in book clubs, fitness challenges, investment groups and informal girlfriend groups. Many of us form "best friend" bonds with another woman and like Betty and Wilma, Lucy and Ethel, and Mary and Rhoda, stand by one another through all of real life's comedies and tragedies.

Over the course of our lives, our friendships, especially with women become increasingly important. Illness, divorce, the empty nest, our parents' deaths, loss of a spouse or other significant relationship changes are inevitable as we age. "It is our friends who keep us anchored and grounded amid the sea of changes within us and around us," says Patricia Gottlieb Shapiro in her book, *Heart to Heart: Deepening Women's Friendships at Midlife*. Unfortunately, for many of us, our friendships get put low on our list of priorities, robbing us of a significant buffer against sorrow and stress.

The Changing Nature of Relationships

Are your relationships stable or have they changed over time? Some people spend their entire lives in the same neighborhood. Others may have moved many times. Some may have the same friends that they grew up with. Others may have cultivated very different relationships throughout their lives. Some have circles that center around family ties or couple relationships. Others have small – or no – families or lose their couples friends in divorce or the death of a spouse. Some have very large friendship circles; others prefer smaller ones. Friends may disappear from our lives for many years and then return.

Loss

As we age, we may begin to lose friends to death, relocation or incapacitating health situations. It is important to mourn the loss of these relationships as well as to honor them.

Evaluate each relationship as changes occur. Relocation and health issues can be overcome if you really want to maintain the bond. Can you overcome distance through internet or phone connections? Many women have ongoing weekly calls with groups of high school or college friends.

Are you willing and able to find work-arounds for physical changes? Your friends may no longer be as mobile or able to engage in activities for as long, but you may find new ways of connecting. They may have moved into assisted living, but still eager to host visitors – or have you join them for a field trip.

Some of us will lose some mental acuity as we age. For some, dementia or Alzheimer's will create changes and perhaps limitations. Natalie Tucker Miller, President of Ageless-Sages Publishing, talks about maintaining relationships with elders. She finds great joy in spending time with Elders – and it begins with accepting people where they are. Can you accept your friends where they are? Can you share memories or a good laugh without other expectations?

What, if any accommodations are you wiling to make to overcome geographic limitations?

_____

_____

_____

_____

_____

_____

_____

What, if any, accommodations are you willing to make to overcome health limitations or altered mental status?

_____

_____

_____

_____

_____

_____

_____

_____

Developing New Relationships

Sometimes, it becomes important to expand our circles. It can seem harder to make new friends in adulthood. For many people, school friends, workplace friends or the parents of their children's classmates and friends form the center of friendship networks. These are the people we see every day. We have a lot in common with them and for some, these relationships are enough to fill all their relationship needs for life.

For others, those work-school-parenting relationships are not sustained. We may find that we don't have much in common any more if we have not found other mutual interests over time. As one friend put it, "I've known these women since my kids were born. I love them to death, but sometimes I want to talk about more than lip gloss and grandchildren."

There are many ways to develop new relationships and perhaps a few caveats. Although these new relationships can become deep and meaningful, there may be differences between them and relationships developed early in life that are worth noting. If you are joining a group with prior relationships of any length, you may feel like you're playing catch-up. There will always be history there – in jokes you don't get, rituals that my not make sense to you, a way of short-handing things that you don't quite get. Be prepared to ignore this, knowing that you will add your own chapters to the group's history. If you're feeling left out, ask for some background. Some members of intact groups may seem to warm up to you slowly. Just give them time.

Finding activity-related groups is an excellent way to meet new people. One wonderful group is *The Transition Network*, for women over fifty, www.thetransitionnetwork.org sponsors monthly meetings, special events, and peer groups. The peer groups are a wonderful way to create a close circle of friends. Some groups have continued for decades.

Most religious organizations have a variety of groups organized around special interests. Community groups, cultural organizations including museums, theaters, wildlife conservancies and botanical gardens all have member groups. Membership in the *Theater Development Fund*, www.tdf.org in New York City, and similar organizations throughout the country can lead to new relationships. The discounted seats tend to be in blocks, so over time many TDF members develop friendships.

Volunteer! There are so many organizations that need your help that it is possible to give as much or as little time as you want helping every imaginable cause while expanding your network.

What are some ways in which you can create new relationships?

_____

_____

_____

_____

_____

_____

_____

_____

Our Relationship with Pets

When we think of relationships, we may automatically go to the humans in our lives, forgetting the significant role pets also play. For some, animal companions may become more important than human ones. According to *Age Erasers for Women*, pets are good for health and longevity. Pet owners have lower levels of blood pressure and cholesterol than non-owners - even when both groups had the same heart-harming habits, like smoking or a high-fat diet. Another study showed that your dog may play a role in protecting you from heart disease in the first place. The researchers speculate that it is the loving, uncritical presence of pets that lowers physical responses to stress.

> Pets are humanizing. They remind us we have an obligation and responsibility to preserve and nurture and care for all life.
> **James Cromwell**

Dogs, cats, birds - the choice is yours - whether you decide to walk a dog, stroke a cat or talk to a canary, you're getting love, easing stress and bolstering your heart health.

Who Can You Trust? Identifying a Support Network

Our need for a support network never changes. Research tells us that maintaining strong connections with others, whether family or friends, is highly correlated to longevity. Who is in your network? How often do you review your support system?

'Tis not enough to help the feeble up, but to support them after.
William Shakespeare

All of us need support, but we don't always think about where that support comes from. Sometimes, we make the mistake of thinking that we can get all the support we need – no matter what kind – from one or two key people or even just from our pets. The problem with this is that people can get burnt out over time and pets can't meet all our needs. Take a good look at your personal network. Think of your support network as consisting of four different roles. Here are the roles that make up a good support network:

Comforters

A comforter is the first person you call when things aren't going well. Comforters give you all the sympathy you need – and nothing but sympathy. They make a pot of tea or open a bottle of wine or find something chocolate and sit down to listen and listen and listen. They offer you words of comfort. They are willing to hear the same story hundreds of times if that's what it takes. A comforter will not try to fix things or offer advice. They just offer you all the unconditional support you need whenever you need it.

Clarifiers

A clarifier is an expert at sorting things out. Clarifiers help you get at what is going on beneath the surface. They probe to find the real problem and help you get a clear idea of what you want to do about it. You can bring any situation to clarifiers and they will ask you questions, listen, ask more questions, pose hypothetical situations, help develop solutions, and, finally, help you pick the solution that will work best for you. When you can't figure out what went wrong – or right – or what to do next, sit down with a clarifier and work through the situation.

Confronters

A confronter will not let you get away with a thing. Confronters remind you of your commitments and push and push until you meet them. If you mention a goal to them, they will ask for a progress report every time you see them. You may not always like your confronters, but they are essential for all of us who have a tendency to procrastinate. They don't accept excuses and they don't give up until you finish what you started.

Cheerleaders

A cheerleader offers unconditional support all the time. Cheerleaders will tell you how great you are even if all you did was get out of bed in the morning. Cheerleaders are relentlessly enthusiastic about even your smallest accomplishment. They urge you on to do whatever you want to do, not by pushing, but by applauding every effort and reminding you just how wonderful you are.

Each of the roles in a support network is distinct and each should be performed by a different person. Even better, by two people. Make yourself a chart like the one on the next page.

	Home	Work
Comforter		
Clarifier		
Confronter		
Cheerleader		

Fill in at least one name (two is better) in each box. When you need support, stop for a minute to think about what you need most. Call someone in that box first. Move on to others as needed. Keep this chart handy and review it every six months. Support is a two-way street. Who do you support? In what way? Make a second chart that represents that network.

A friendship can weather most things and thrive in thin soil; but it needs a little mulch of letters and phone calls and small, silly presents every so often - just to save it from drying out completely.

Pam Brown

Relationships Questions

How will I create a family of choice or support network?

Do my relationships propel me forward or hold me back?

What do I want/need from my friends and family?

Where will I find support when I need it?

How will I remain in connection with others?

How will I create space for myself?

How will I maintain my family of choice or support network?

How close do I want to remain to my family?

Can I sustain the same number of relationships I have had?

Do I need to replace losses or increase my circle?

How am I creating and sustaining space for myself?

How near do I want to be to my remaining family and/or children?

How will I make living decisions with my spouse or life partner?

How will I deal with the loss of significant relationships?

What relationships do I want to sustain?

How will I maintain space for myself?

Meaningful Work Blueprint Playbook

A step-by-step guide to creating a job, a business or volunteer opportunities

Meaningful Work

Work adds meaning to our lives. It increases satisfaction; it provides a way to give back; it provides a way to continue to learn and grow – if you have found work that is right for you. This blueprint takes you through a process in which you will identify your skills and group them into broad categories that will help you explore specific areas in which you might want to contribute and help you identify the skills you most want to use.

In this blueprint, "work" is used as a broad term to include paid and unpaid experiences. If you are a homemaker, you are working. If you are a caretaker for relatives, you are working. If you volunteer, you are working.

In the space below, describe your favorite job and what made it special.

_____

_____

_____

_____

_____

_____

_____

_____

_____

_____

_____

_____

Looking Back: A Starting Point

In the Vision Blueprint, you wrote a eulogy that gave you a picture of what you wanted out of life. That may provide enough information for this blueprint. If you want more detail, however, take some time to write a life history. Your life history paints a picture of all the things you have done, not just in terms of experiences and emotions, but in terms of skills. In fact, it's a sort of very long résumé. However you choose to organize the information, the more skills that you can identify, the clearer your future direction will be.

Once you have identified all the skills you can, you will be able to group them in a meaningful way that will translate into job categories. John Holland, a career theorist who developed one of the best known and most widely used career inventories, once said that there is no instrument available that is more reliable than simply asking a person what they want to do. Similarly, there is no skills test more reliable – and certainly none more individualized – than the one you will construct for yourself based on the facts of your life.

Review the skills you have. What are all the examples in your life of using these skills? What else was going on at that time? Were you happy or sad? Feeling productive? Self-confident? What skills were you using at periods of frustration? Were you using them to cope and work through the frustration, or did the skills themselves cause frustration?

Career Areas

Here is an example of what skills organizing, or coding, might look like. It's an excerpt from a life history. Lee is a training manager with a major transportation company. Here is her description of her job, with skills shown in bold:

> I **train** a variety of courses, including basic **supervisory and managerial skills**. I helped **develop** the

curriculum for both of those programs. I also developed **sexual harassment awareness** training. I enjoy **working with people**. I like **speaking with a lot of different people** and usually touch base with most of my colleagues every day. I think color is very important, and all of my materials are color-coded. I like to **use** a lot of **color** and pictures in my training materials.

I like **making** my **environment pleasant** as well and pay a lot of attention to how my work area looks. I usually have a color theme. Color is important in my wardrobe, too. **I like putting together interesting combinations**. **If you believe** that two colors work together, **you can make everyone else believe** it, too!

I am interested in **career development**. I've been part of the

selection committee for the Future Managers Program for several years. I also work with a college program hosted by the organization and serve as a **mentor** to a high school student. My mentoring experience has helped me **develop mentoring programs** within the organization.

Recently, I've become involved with **training middle managers**. I've learned how to teach **problem solving and decision making** and have expanded my skills as a **facilitator**. I will be helping this group **design and run an annual conference**. I'll be able to use my experience in teaching **presentation skills** to help them become better speakers for the conference.

I also volunteer as an **announcer for a cable television program** and do a little **consulting** in the areas of **performance management** and **stress management**.

As you begin to narrow your search for meaningful work that appeals to you, you may want to select general career categories to think about. There are many interest inventories or other instruments that will categorize this information for you, based on your expressed interests, but you can do a better job yourself. Who knows better than you what your preferences are? Now you'll need to organize all that information in ways that make it most useful to you. There are six categories here that work for most women, but you may want to create your own. Feel free. This is just a starting point.

The categories:

Artist

Expression is essential to your work life, whether it is visual or verbal. You need to express feelings and ideas in a tangible way through writing or speaking or pictorial representation. You need to create new things and do this best in an unstructured setting. You need to be free to express your ideas and prefer a certain level of spontaneity, change, and constant challenge so that your mind can leap from one project to the next. You may work better on your own than with others. You are sensitive to the needs of others. You use your creativity and artistic talents to solve problems.

Practical/Realist

Getting concrete things done is important to you. You are at your best when dealing with tangible problems and being given the tools and authority to accomplish things. You enjoy working with your hands. You may like taking things apart

168

just to see how they work or tinkering with things to see if you can repair them. You may prefer work that takes you outdoors, where you can make the best use of your need to remain physically active.

Investigator

Most of all, you need to be able to figure out how things work. You have an inquisitive mind and are always asking questions (although maybe just to yourself) and looking for connections between ideas and events. You see patterns easily and are able to synthesize information from a variety of sources into a coherent whole. You thrive on abstract problems. Although you are often energized by others, you do your best work independently.

Systematic Detailer

You are the one who always notices the loose ends and fatal flaws. You need a great deal of information and are also the best person to organize all that information into a logical flow and badger others to plug up any gaps. You thrive on detail work. You solve problems by identifying the applicable rules and following them. You are reliable, so others depend on you for support and assistance.

Influencer

You are a born leader and need to have some sort of following – whether it's clients or students. You are energetic and enthusiastic and enjoy being surrounded by lots of other people. You are also very goal oriented. You have many opinions and love to share them. You tend to be a quick thinker and are excellent with language. You are willing to take risks in order to solve problems.

Helper/Social Purpose

You are sensitive and supportive. Many people come to you with their problems because you are such a sympathetic listener and because you are so understanding. If you talk with people long enough, you become very clear about how their problems might be solved.

In your skills organization, if you find that you've leaned heavily toward Helper/Social Purpose or Systematic Detailer, you might want to think a little about your responses. Most women, by nature or role, do a lot of these things. Your responses, therefore, may be more due to your nurturing inclination than naturally developed or preferred talents. Then again, these may be the gifts that you most prefer to use. Ask yourself just one question to be sure. Is this what you want to do more of or a role you'd like to expand away from?

Which skills category or categories best describes you?

_____

_____

_____

_____

_____

_____

Now, here is a partial list of Lee's skills in categories, drawn from the job description above. Note how there is a specific example wherever possible. Some skills may be listed in more than one category.

Artist
announcer for a cable television program
consulting – creating new programs; synthesizing ideas
presentation skills
develop mentoring programs

Practical/Realist
consulting – creating practical applications of skills
problem solving and decision making

Investigator
consulting – figuring out what is happening in an organization
problem solving and decision making

Influencer

consulting – convincing people

announcer for a cable television program

career development

presentation skills

Helper/Social Purpose

consulting – helping people improve their abilities

career development

presentation skills

develop mentoring programs

Weighting Your Skills

After you have listed all of your skills in these areas, go back and assign weights to each skill in terms of level of use, level of ability, and level of enjoyment.

How high is your level of ability?

    5 – I 'm great at this!

    4 – I'm better than most.

    3 – I'm just about average.

    2 – This is really not one of my best things.

1 – Are you sure you want to let me touch this?

How often do you use this skill?

    5 – About as often as I breathe.

    4 – Most of my time centers around this.

    3 – Maybe half the time or a little less.

    2 – Often enough to remember how to use it.

    1 – What skill was that?

How much do you enjoy using this skill?

    5 – I would probably pay to be able to do this.

    4 – Few things in life make me happier.

    3 – Take it or leave it.

    2 – Maybe someone else would like to give it a try?

    1 – It sets my teeth on edge.

Here are Lee's weighted artistic skills:

Skill	Level	Use	Enjoy
A – announcer for a cable television program	4	2	4
A – consulting – creating new programs; synthesizing ideas	3	4	2
A – presentation skills	5	1	5
A – develop mentoring programs	3	3	2

Start to put your top skills – those in which you are most proficient, like best, and use with some regularity – together. Add to this group skills you think you would enjoy developing more fully. Use this as the basis for your job search. You can use career guides or the *Dictionary of Occupational Titles* to locate some job possibilities.

Be imaginative. Look at your skills in clusters, and think of how they might be used. It may take a combination of paid and unpaid employment – or you may start your own business. The largest growing group of new entrepreneurs is women over 40.

Weighted Skills List
Skills Categories

When you have finished the sort, you will be able to divide your skills into four categories:

Display shelf – skills to be used most

Building blocks – skills or behaviors that can be developed

Recycle – skills or behaviors that can be used differently

Trash heap – skills or behaviors that we want to throw away

Weighted Skills List

Skill	Level	Use	Enjoy

Skill	Level	Use	Enjoy

Display Shelf	**Building Blocks**
Recycle	**Trash Heap**

Researching Possibilities

Read everything you can that will help you have a better understanding of what work is right for you. Start with the basic "This is what a _____ does" information that you can find in any library. Then branch out. Look for magazine and newspaper articles about the field. Read fiction, too – sometimes marvelous details about a field emerge this way. Just one Patricia Cornwell mystery, for example, should give you a pretty clear idea of what a forensic coroner might do. Read biographies. How did someone else get into a field that interests you?

Interview people. Most people are delighted to talk to you about their jobs. Find out why these people like their work. What are the frustrations as well as the satisfactions? What is their career history? Did they receive formal training? Where? Did they select this type of work or fall into it? Did they fall into another job that eventually led them to this one?

When you interview people, ask them who else they think you should speak to or what else you should do in the way of research. Find out what they read – what journals, what trade papers. Find out if there are conferences or professional meetings. Often, there are some open sessions that outsiders can attend.

Find out if this is work you could try out as a volunteer or, if special training is required, if there are related jobs that might help you get a feel for the work. Maybe you could do volunteer work for the professional organization. What better way to make contacts?

Don't think about just one job – learn to think about a series of experiences.

Generally, skills can be transferred to a number of different occupations. If you can think of your skills as portable – a term that is becoming increasingly popular as people have a series of jobs rather than one-company careers, you should be able to identify a number of different ways to combine those skills in a number of different fields.

Finding the right work is a creative process. As with any creative process, it sometimes takes a flight from reality to suggest real, practical ideas to us. Or, just maybe, that fantasy isn't so unrealistic after all. Many years ago, I used life histories as part of a career-planning course. Each woman, after completing her life history and skills analysis, selected three alternate careers. Ideally, these were jobs that she never thought about doing. The choices could be real or they could be total fantasy.

One woman who completed this process was a woman in her early 60s. She was working as a teacher's aide and felt that she was too old to do anything else. Then she remembered a story her coach had told about her own grandmother, who, at the age of 80, had taken a job caring for an elderly woman. One of her alternate career choices was to become a politician. She decided that she had nothing to lose and applied for the community board. She got that appointment and a year later won a seat in the state assembly. So much for old age and unrealistic dreams!

What's Important?

Which skills do you want to use? Which skills are important to keep? Which could you easily give up? For this exercise, you'll need to develop a personal vision of yourself at work. Make index cards or strips of paper for each of your skills. Sort through them to reduce the pile to no more than 30 skills that are important to you. Now try to reduce the pile to 20.

The purpose of this exercise is to identify a set of core skills – the ones that are an essential part of your being. Without these skills, you feel incomplete – as if a limb has been amputated. We all have many skills that we can use and do use, but few that are part of our core. Meaningful work is built around using those skills.

Some people find this next step painful. Take the 20 skills remaining (or more if you absolutely couldn't discard them). You're going to have to give up skills that are important to you. Remember that this is only an exercise – not your life. When you've gone as far as you can in the process, you can take skills back.

Arrange your skill cards in priority order, number 1 being the skill that is most important to you. If, as you work through this exercise, you begin to feel differently about the order of skills, just change it. Now, begin to discard skills, one at a time. Start with number 20 – the least essential skill in the group. Reduce the pile as far as you can. Stop removing skills when you feel uncomfortable about giving up anything else. Try to reduce the pile to a number somewhere between 5 and 8. These are your core skills. If they are not utilized in your paid employment, you will need to broaden your horizons to include other productive activities that provide you with opportunities to use them.

Without these, you will always feel stifled and less than you can be.

Vision

Now concentrate on these remaining skills. Envision yourself using them. Where are you? Who is there? How do you feel? What is giving you satisfaction in this experience?

Résumé Writing

Use your skills analysis to guide you in writing your résumé. Although you have a specific set of facts to work with, there are many ways to organize those facts. Your résumé should reflect those achievements you are proudest of and should point in the direction of the kind of work you've already envisioned yourself doing.

Organizing the Job Campaign

Locating work that has meaning to you requires a major commitment of time and energy. You are trying to find either the right paid employment or a combination of paid and unpaid work that will give you life satisfaction.

The Sales Pitch – Interviewing

Employment specialists will tell you that you have three minutes to make the sale.

People are all around you offering opportunities. Keep your eyes open. Be aware. Take what's offered – don't try to make it into something that it isn't.

A Patchwork Life

Bettina Aptheker wrote that women are by nature thrifty and can't bear waste. They save little scraps of fabric and piece them together to form something both useful and beautiful. Many women fashion extraordinary careers and extraordinary lives in this way. They construct their own families from pieces of other families. They construct meaningful careers from a variety of jobs or jobs and volunteer work.

Doris has retired after many years in social work and training management. She knew that she would be bored, so she immediately looked for some sort of part-time work – paid or unpaid. She found an organization that helps immigrants learn English. Among their services is an entertainment bureau that provides low-cost or free tickets to program participants and volunteers. Doris is able to support her lifelong love of concerts and theater at very little cost to herself this way.

Doris still needed something else to do. She had an outlet for her excellent administrative skills in her volunteer work but wanted paid employment as well. She was interested in using her social work skills, but knew she did not want the demands of a social work position. She found a part-time position with the courts that allows her to work with clients on a very limited basis and provides her with a small supplemental income.

But Doris has taken her patchwork skills beyond organizing her employment and entertainment. She has applied these same skills to creating a family. Although Doris had a series of satisfying relationships, she had never married and had no children. She felt the need to have family connections and to nurture children, although not necessarily the need to parent. Her sister had married and raised two children, and through the years Doris had an ongoing relationship with them. When she was busy with her career and her own social life, this was enough.

As Doris grew older, she wanted a closer connection with her family and with children. By this time, her niece and nephew had grown and had each married. Doris remained close enough to them to have a strong bond with their children and has become "Aunt Dorrie." As a great aunt, she is the favorite relative of six children, all of whom look forward not only to her visits with them, but, as they grow up, to their being able to visit her in New York.

Jane has taken a similar approach to finding work satisfaction outside the boundaries of her regular job. Jane has a relatively unexciting job. The biggest advantage is that she has a fair amount of mental down time between projects. She is able to maintain an active and demanding political life in part because her job requires so little of her mental energy. After years of political activities centering around civil rights, the antiwar movement, and campaigning for freedom for political prisoners, she has recently branched out into neighborhood politics and environmental concerns. She has meetings almost every night and a circle of close friends with whom she has strong personal and political bonds. She has also been able to share a wide range of other interests, including art, music, crafts, and wonderful meals with her fellow activists. While the circle may expand and contract, the core of fellowship remains. Jane is a woman who will never be without purpose or companionship.

What could your life look like? Use the space below to list possibilities.

_____

_____

_____

_____

_____

_____

_____

_____

_____

_____

_____

_____

_____

_____

_____

_____

_____

_____

Ideal Surroundings Blueprint Playbook

A step-by-step guide to identifying your ideal surroundings

Ideal Surroundings

He is the happiest, be he king or peasant, who finds peace in his home.
Johann Wolfgang von Goethe

Isn't it important to decide where you want to spend your life? You wouldn't decide on a house without knowing where it was. Your surroundings have an influence on every other aspect of your life. There are two areas to consider: where you live and what your living space is like.

Do you have a home that makes you feel comfortable? Do you want to invite people into your home? Can you live the life you desire in your current space? Do you have access to what you want and need?

What's important to you in finding the ideal community, in selecting and furnishing a living space, in bringing people into your life? Is this a decision you can make alone or is there a life partner who will join you in making these decisions?

Before we begin to work through the components of creating a blueprint for your ideal surroundings, take a few minutes to do a little dreaming.

My Ideal Home

Find a comfortable space. Sit back, relax, and let your mind wander. Imagine yourself sitting in the living room of your ideal home. What does the room look like? How large is it? How is the room furnished? Where are you sitting? What is on the walls around you? Look out of the window. What do you see? How does this room make you feel?

Now, walk around your home. How many rooms are there? Stop in each one long enough to capture the details. What are your favorite features in each room? Your favorite objects?

Where is your home? Is this a house or an apartment? Are you in a city? A suburb? The country? Near water? Look around. What makes you smile?

Open your eyes and write down as much as you can remember:

_____

_____

_____

_____

_____

_____

_____

_____

_____

_____

_____

_____

_____

_____

_____

_____

Now that you have an overall picture, let's develop a blueprint item by item. Here are some areas to consider and a few questions to get you started:

Climate

Do you prefer a warm climate or a cool one? How are you affected by humidity? Does very dry air bother you? Is it important to be near water? Lake, river, or ocean?

Culture

How important, if at all, is it for you to have access to cultural events? How do you define culture? For some, museums, concerts, theater, and dance may be crucial. Others may want a good multiplex or proximity to their favorite team. Some may need good cable access; others want libraries.

Cost

Where can you afford to live? How much do you want to spend on your surroundings? What are the costs associated with different types of housing (initial and recurring)?

Community

Are the size and composition of your community important to you? Some prefer urban bustle; others may want age-restricted, gated communities. Some want many activities; others prefer to be on their own.

Politics

Some communities seem to be hotbeds of political activity, while others avoid anything political. Political beliefs may also vary. How important is it to you to be surrounded by people with similar political and social values?

People

Who will your neighbors be? How frequently do you want to interact with them? Will you want to live alone? In shared space? In community with others?

Physical Environment

The factors here are wide-ranging. Some of them overlap with climate and cultural concerns. Do you want a densely or sparsely populated area? A single or multifamily dwelling? How will stairs or a parking space factor into your plans? Do you want lots of space or something more compact? A garden? Community facilities?

Personal Safety

What concerns, if any, do you have for your safety that might influence your choice of surroundings? This might include need for a security system or doorman or proximity to a parking space or public transportation.

Work

Will you be working or volunteering? How will commuting factor into your planning? Will you need access to transportation and services at nontraditional hours?

Education

Do you have plans to continue your education? Will you have access? Physical or virtual?

Leisure Activities

How do you enjoy spending your leisure time? What will you require in your surroundings to accommodate your leisure needs? Access to a golf club? Museums? A botanical garden or nature preserve? Just a Lazy Boy and a remote? An excellent gym?

Transportation

How will you travel? Do you need good public transportation? Access to an international airport? Bike paths and good sidewalks?

Health Care

Are there health issues that might limit where you choose to live? These might include not only treatment needs and access to specialized hospital facilities but also limitations imposed by your insurance coverage.

> *Home is a name, a word, it is a strong one; stronger than magician ever spoke, or spirit ever answered to, in the strongest conjuration.*
> *Charles Dickens*

Personal Definitions

Each of the areas that comprise surroundings may mean something different to each person. Use the spaces provided to create personal definitions of each of the areas. List as many factors as you can think of. Blank space has been provided in case you want to add something to the list.

Climate

_____

_____

_____

_____

_____

_____

_____

Culture

_____

_____

_____

_____

_____

_____

Cost

_____

_____

_____

_____

_____

_____

Community

_____

_____

_____

_____

_____

_____

_____

Politics

_____

_____

_____

_____

_____

_____

_____

People

_____

_____

_____

_____

_____

_____

_____

Physical Environment

_____

_____

_____

_____

_____

_____

_____

Personal Safety

_____

_____

_____

_____

_____

_____

Work

_____

_____

_____

_____

_____

_____

Education

_____

_____

_____

_____

_____

_____

Leisure Activities

_____

_____

_____

_____

_____

_____

Transportation

_____

_____

_____

_____

_____

_____

_____

Health Care

_____

_____

_____

_____

_____

_____

_____

Wants and Needs

By creating definitions, you now have a clearer idea of what each of these areas comprises for you – the most important factors in each area. This is an especially important step if you are planning with a partner. Your personal definitions will make it more clear what factors you will want to consider in each area. For example, your definition of transportation might be having extensive public transportation or easy access to a major airport or ease of renting a car for short periods of time. These definitions will help you determine your wants and needs.

A state arises, as I conceive, out of the needs of mankind; no one is self-sufficing, but all of us have many wants.
Plato

Wants

In the spaces below, list all the factors you want for each area.

Climate

_____

_____

_____

_____

_____

_____

Culture

_____

_____

_____

_____

_____

_____

_____

Cost

_____

_____

_____

_____

_____

_____

_____

Community

_____

_____

_____

_____

_____

_____

_____

Politics

_____

_____

_____

_____

_____

_____

_____

People

_____

_____

_____

_____

_____

_____

_____

Physical Environment

_____

_____

_____

_____

_____

_____

_____

Personal Safety

_____

_____

_____

_____

_____

_____

Work

_____

_____

_____

_____

_____

_____

Needs

Go back over the lists one more time and highlight, circle, or underline one or two factors for each section that are make-or-break for you. Use the space below to list those factors. They are your needs, and just as you would not accept a blueprint for a house that was missing a necessary element, like bathrooms or access to the second floor, so too you do not want to accept an ideal location that is missing elements that are crucial to you.

List your needs in the space below. You may not have needs in every category.

Climate

_____

_____

_____

Culture

_____

_____

_____

Cost

_____

_____

_____

Community

_____

_____

_____

Politics

_____

_____

_____

People

_____

_____

_____

Physical Environment

_____

_____

_____

Personal Safety

_____

_____

_____

Work

_____

_____

_____

Education

_____

_____

_____

Leisure Activities

_____

_____

_____

Transportation

_____

_____

_____

Health Care

_____

_____

_____

Now you're ready to look at your entire list. Go back to your dream surroundings description and review it in terms of the lists you have made. Use the spaces below to create a short description for each category that includes your needs and your top two or three wants.

Climate

_____

_____

_____

_____

_____

_____

Culture

_____

_____

_____

_____

_____

_____

_____

Cost

_____

_____

_____

_____

_____

_____

_____

Community

_____

_____

_____

_____

_____

_____

_____

Politics

_____

_____

_____

_____

_____

_____

_____

People

_____

_____

_____

_____

_____

_____

Physical Environment

_____

_____

_____

_____

_____

_____

Personal Safety

_____

_____

_____

_____

_____

_____

_____

Work

_____

_____

_____

_____

_____

_____

_____

Education

_____

_____

_____

_____

_____

_____

Leisure Activities

_____

_____

_____

_____

_____

_____

Transportation

_____

_____

_____

_____

_____

_____

_____

Health Care

_____

_____

_____

_____

_____

_____

_____

Using the questions on the next page to spark your thinking and the wants and needs you have identified, you will have created a blueprint for your ideal surroundings. Use that blueprint as a guide to identifying communities that meet your wants and needs.

Ideal Surroundings Blueprint – Questions

Who will I live with or live near?

Can I live with my family?

How near do I want to be to my family?

Do I prefer to live alone or with others?

How near do I want to be to my friends?

How does geography limit or enhance my relationships?

How will I make living decisions with my spouse or life partner?

What environment best supports raising a family?

What physical criteria apply?

Do I prefer urban, suburban, or rural?

How do my physical surroundings reflect my true self?

What amenities will I want in my surroundings?

How does my environment support my life goals?

What will I do if my spouse or significant other needs continuous care?

What will I do if I can no longer live independently?

What type of supported living (if any) is right for me?

What are my financial concerns?

Do I want to rent, or can I consider buying a home?

What can I afford?

What will I do if my spouse or significant other needs continuous care?

What will I do if I can no longer live independently?

What type of supported living (if any) is right for me?

Spirituality Blueprint Playbook

A step-by-step user-friendly guide to exploring Spirit in your ideal life

Dr. Lin Morel for Dr. Susan R. Meyer

Why Think About Spirituality?

We are not human beings having a spiritual experience. We are spiritual beings having a human experience.

Teilhard de Chardin, priest, philosopher, mystic, geologist

Once upon a time, many many years ago, I had several experiences that awakened in me the awareness that I was a spiritual being having a human experience. That awakening was nurtured in a most unusual way - through the martial arts and the guidance of my judo teacher, Gene Waddell. His loving kindness and compassion, so freely offered to a challenged teenager in a challenging family, gave me firm ground to grow strong.

Today I am a fifth degree black belt in karate, minister, spiritual director and consultant. My human experience growing up was radically changed as a result of a glimpse into the greater reality of who I was. This perspective has helped me navigate the most amazing, challenging and fulfilling life.

A simple working definition of spiritual is that which expresses the highest part of your nature and religion as the frame through which you might choose to express this nature. You could call higher nature our Soul, Spirit or Divinity. Spirituality can be known apart from religion, although religion is not really separate from spirituality. It's fascinating that most religions agree that spirit exists "outside" as well as "inside" - and can be made known (and experienced) through a loving heart.

However you define it, everyone has a need for connection with something greater than themselves and some opportunity for self-renewal. For some, this may be organized religion and regular attendance at a church, temple, mosque, or ashram. For others, this may involve private rituals of regular prayer, chanting or meditation. For still others, this may involve spending time in nature.

Leider and Shapiro, in *Claiming Your Place at the Fire*, see spirituality as closely aligned with purpose. Understanding and developing your spiritual nature becomes a prerequisite to defining your life's purpose. Taking time for the spirit and for self-renewal is also closely aligned with stress management and wellness. Meditation helps control elevated blood pressure.

Thomas Moore stresses the importance of caring for the soul in his book of the same name. He defines soul as, "the font of who we are," and goes on to say, "... and yet it is far beyond our capacity to devise and control. We can cultivate, tend, enjoy, and participate in the things of the soul, but we can't outwit it or manage it or shape it to the designs of a willful ego." He feels it is this care of the soul that gave rise to the extraordinary creativity of the Renaissance in Italy.

John Morgan, in his book, *The Existential Quest of Meaning*, adds that "This ability of persons to self-determine his or her life is perhaps the most fundamental example of the spiritual nature of the person. He says, "This is the one chance we have to be the particular person we know that we can be. It is this chance to self-determine that guides and shapes millions of lives, whether it is named spirituality or not."

What is Your Authentic Self?

Our Soul's qualities are love, peace, joy, bliss, courageousness and a deep abiding knowingness that cannot be shaken by events in our life. Our authentic self is what is real. That realness is seen and expressed through the eyes of loving and Godness or Goodness. Although we cannot see electricity or loving, we know it is present because of the results.

Defining Spirituality for Yourself

What does the word Spirit mean to you?

_____

_____

_____

_____

_____

_____

Does the word Spirit bring up anxiety or positive feelings? Does it puzzle you?

_____

_____

_____

_____

_____

What do you think of when you think of a spiritual person?

_____

_____

_____

_____

_____

_____

What are your judgments (positive and/or negative) about spirituality?

_____

_____

_____

_____

_____

_____

Are you religious or spiritual? What does that difference mean to you?

_____

_____

_____

_____

_____

_____

What does it mean to encounter Spirit?

_____

_____

_____

_____

_____

_____

Describe a time when you encountered Spirit. What was your experience?

_____

_____

_____

_____

_____

_____

Expanding Your Spirituality

Have you ever used a guide to support you as you answer these questions? This is the province of spiritual exploration with a mentor. Spirituality is the process of looking inward to discover who you are as a spiritual being. How do you think spirituality could support you in your life?

_____

_____

_____

_____

_____

_____

What you think you might be missing without a spiritual connection?

_____

_____

_____

_____

_____

_____

Here are more areas of exploration for seekers on a spiritual path.

What would happen if you were connected to a source of peace and wisdom? How would your life change?

_____

_____

_____

_____

_____

_____

How would your life be improved if you let go of worry and fear? Anger? Guilt?

_____

_____

_____

_____

_____

_____

What might stand between you and a relationship with the Spirit within?

_____

_____

_____

_____

_____

_____

Does that block protect you in some way? From what? What would happen if you let it go?

_____

_____

_____

_____

_____

_____

What would your life look like if you had a partnership with the Spirit within?

_____

_____

_____

_____

_____

Applying a Spiritual Perspective in Your Life

A spiritual perspective offers other viewpoints and solutions to your daily challenges. Here are two case studies that illustrate the power of a exploring the power of applied spirituality to real life situations.

I had a client once who came to me seeking a divorce after almost 54 years of marriage. During our time together she was quite agitated, saying "I can't stand him. I hate him. I can't stand to be in the same room with him. I want a divorce." I sent her home and asked her to say nine words SILENTLY every time she thought of or spoke with her husband.

What do you think these words were?

_____

_____

The nine words are: I love you. God bless you. Peace. Be Still.

When you read this, what is your initial reaction?

_____

_____

_____

_____

_____

When she returned for her follow-up meeting, she announced, "You ruined my plans. I remember why I married him and I no longer want to divorce him. She asked me, "How could something so simple work so quickly?"

What do you think shifted as she turned her focus to those nine words?

_____

_____

_____

_____

_____

_____

Think of an area in your life where you are feeling betrayed, disappointed, abandoned or negative about a person. They could be living or dead.

Write it down.

_____

_____

_____

_____

_____

If you are willing, apply the nine words to the situation you addressed above. Spend at least three weeks (or more) with this little experiment. If you can't bring yourself to say all of the words, that's fine. Just pick something that is symbolic for you to say, and do it daily, even if it doesn't feel true. Keeping a journal will let you follow your process.

_____

_____

_____

_____

_____

_____

When I did this little experiment in 1993, I'd been estranged from my family for 17 years. I did it as part of a research project into the impact of "inner" work and its effect on outer situations. I chose my younger sister as my subject. I also began to call her and/or send her one note or card a month. As an after thought, I added my aunt, my brother and my older sister (the living members of my immediate family). I did nothing for them other than say, "I love you. God bless you. Peace. Be Still at least one time a day."

Just six weeks later, on Thanksgiving, every member of my family called! This had not happened during the previous 17 years! They said things like, "I've been thinking about you a lot," " I wanted to call and say I miss you and love you", etc. Today I have a great relationship with them, all because I got curious about my connection with my inner spirit and how it could help me dissolve something I'd not been able to do on my own.

Chances are you will notice some shift in your relationship with the person you use as your subject. The results don't really matter. What I discovered was that I became more loving and compassionate to them where they "lived inside of me." The icing on the cake was that I actually healed my relationship with them in the physical.

Self-renewal

Tending the spirit can also be as simple as taking time for self-renewal. This is the time we spend nurturing ourselves taking a break from day-to-day responsibilities and focusing on what we need. The following is a short list of quick ways to renew yourself. What can you add?

Take a walk alone or with your partner. Some couples report that this time together is what keeps their relationship vibrant.

Solitary walks not only improve your health, they provide
valuable time to shed the cares of the day or to focus on solving
a problem.

Find something beautiful every day. Appreciation of the wonders
around us renews the spirit.

Tell yourself that you love yourself. One woman starts every day
by standing in front of her mirror, giving herself a big hug, and
saying, "Not bad for a little (insert self-descriptive phrase) girl!"

Smile often. You'll enjoy the reward of seeing your smile
mirrored in others. Smiling is good for our facial muscles and
studies prove that smiling enhances problem-solving skills.

Take a bubble bath. Go all out and light candles if you want.
Those old Calgon commercials were right.

Learn to power nap. Spend ten to fifteen minutes stretched out
on your bed in absolute quiet.

Put on your favorite CD and sing along as loud as you want to.

Dance.

Write a note to someone you have been meaning to get in touch
with. There's something wonderful about taking pen to paper.

Look at your photo albums. Most of us fill up albums and never
look back.

Write in your journal.

Light a candle and stare into the flame for 10 minutes.

The Divine is not something high above us. It is in heaven, it is in earth, it is inside us.

Morihei Usheiba, founder of Aikido, The Way of Peace

Master Tips for Living a Life of Joy

The heart is the perfection of the whole organism. Therefore the principles of the power of perception and the soul's ability to nourish itself must lie in the heart.

Aristotle

Take a Heart/Breath Break

Conscious breathing does wonders to calm you down when your mind or emotions have got the better of you. Begin to pay attention and notice when you hold your breath.

I spent years holding my breath. I knew what to do, yet in spite of my best efforts, I held my breath. I still do when I am overtired or upset. What I discovered was that when I unwilling to experience my feelings I hold my breath. Feelings are your children, and deserve loving. The simple act of acknowledging your emotions (as an observer) is often enough to dissipate them.

The following will help you gently connect with your heart and your emotions. It will also help you re-energize your body. There's no special way to do it, other than doing it.

Imagine you are whatever is agitating you into your heart. Now exhale it out the back of your heart. Think of something you love, now breathe that in and exhale out your back. Relax your shoulders and let the tension flow through and out of you.

It's deceptively simple. You can also do this when you have a physical, emotional or mental challenge. Put the loving in your breath, and breathe compassion into the part that hurts.

Practice Seeing Life Through The Eyes Of Loving.

No matter what the dilemma, loving is the answer.

It's easy to love those who agree with you. It's another to love the person who has robbed you, betrayed you or abandoned you. If in fact the Soul is loving, then that is your greater reality. The task at hand is to choose the reality of your soul and by-pass the negative expression of our false self.

Rest assured, this isn't always easy, although like breathing, it is simple. A simple way to begin putting loving in your life is to start by saying, "I love this."

Even if you don't love the fact that you just got a ticket, you can still say, "I love this." My friend Paul Kaye talks about this in the book *Momentum: Letting Love Lead*.

If you can be grateful for something, you're loving it. One time, my car broke down on the way to an important meeting. I practiced loving the situation and decided that life was perfect anyway. When I got back on the road and turned on the radio, I found that my little detour had kept me out of a massive car accident - right at the time I would have arrived prior to my breakdown. Coincidence? You'll have to decide for yourself. Looking at life through the eyes of loving makes life's detours easier.

Good luck and thank you for exploring spirituality with me! If you would like to receive gifts to support your journey, go to **www.linmorel.com** and click on the gifts section. You can also sign up for an additional complementary e book.

Stay in touch, and let me know how you make out. If you get stuck, I'm available to help you deepen your connection to your Spirit.

Blessings on your journey!

Warmest regards,

Lin Morel

Dr. Lin Morel, 2010 International Coach of the Year, has spent more than four decades studying the field of human consciousness. She is a minister, spiritual director, consultant, speaker, author and mentor to those seeking to apply the principles of heart centered spirituality to their lives and in their work. To learn more about how you can work with Dr. Morel, go to: **http://www.linmorel.com**

Thank you for exploring your relationship with your spirit and spirituality.

Creativity and Self-Expression Blueprint Playbook

A step-by-step guide to adding creativity to your ideal life

Finding Your Inner Creativity

Creativity and the ability to play are crucial components of a good life. This Blueprint will help you think about ways to express your creativity.

How do you express yourself? having some kind of creative outlet plays a big part in having a satisfying life – and, as it turns out, a long one. Karen Springen and Sam Seibert, in a Newsweek article entitled *Don't ever assume your best work is behind you. Creativity often peaks in our later years*. reinforce the need for creative outlets to maintain a youthful attitude, energy, and good mental health. They report that researchers who investigate longevity are discovering that old age can be a peak period for creativity.

You must not for one instant give up the effort to build new lives for yourselves. Creativity means to push open the heavy, groaning doorway to life.

Daisaku Ikeda

Create a list of a dozen activities that you enjoy. What makes you happy? Energized? This will be a starting point for your Blueprint.

_____

_____

_____

_____

_____

_____

_____

_____

_____

_____

Why Think About Creativity?

As we age, experience serves as a rich resource, slowing us down in some ways as we process through larger databases, but providing a fertile ground for growth and creativity. Examples include Laura Ingalls Wilder, who was in her 50's and 60's when she wrote her "Little House" books and Anna (Grandma Moses) Robertson, who sold her first paintings to a collector at 79—and kept at it for the next two decades.

University of Kentucky Prof. David Snowdon, heads the Nun Study, which, since its start in 1986, has documented the health of 678 Roman Catholic nuns over 70 in order to study the relationship between aging and Alzheimer's disease. The sisters engaged in creative activities as simple as puzzles and as complex as painting or writing. Snowden's favorite participant was Sister Esther, who lived to age 107. She took up ceramics at 97 and initially told Snowden that she was too busy for his study.

Creativity is merely a plus name for regular activity. Any activity becomes creative when the doer cares about doing it right, or better.
John Updike

In a study sponsored by the NEA, Dr. Gene Cohen studied three arts programs for Seniors. He found striking differences between the studied group and a control group not involved in the arts. Findings included better health, fewer falls, higher individual sense of control, increased social engagement and greater improvements on each of the depression, loneliness, and morale scales. Related research in psychoneuroimmunology indicates that there is a strong link between increased activity and involvement and sense of well-being.

Creativity is not merely the innocent spontaneity of our youth and childhood; it must also be married to the passion of the adult human being, which is a

passion to live beyond one's death.
Rollo May

One way that researchers measure creativity is by seeing how many different ways an individual can find to use a simple object. On this measure, ability tends to decline after age forty. This doesn't mean that creativity has diminished, however, but merely that it may shift, as intelligence does. Gisela Lebouvie Vief found that individuals engage in more contextual thinking – a practical form of intelligence. Similarly, practical creativity—solving everyday problems — develops as we age. An example is Ben Franklin, who invented the world's first bifocals at 78 based on his own practical vision needs.

Clean out a corner of your mind and creativity will instantly fill it.
  Dee Hock

Our brains continue to develop throughout life. Information is processed through a series of dendrites that connect neuron to neuron. These develop in response to new information or challenges and are strengthened by repeated use. Dr. Gene Cohen, author of "The Creative Age" and director of the Center on Aging, Health and Humanities at George Washington University, has found that this process continues through the life-span. Engaging in creative activities provides one challenge that causes these connections to develop and strengthen.

> *Creativity is a great motivator because it makes people interested in what they are doing. Creativity gives hope that there can be a worthwhile idea. Creativity gives the possibility of some sort of achievement to everyone. Creativity makes life more fun and more interesting.*
> *Edward de Bono*

There are many ways to express your creativity, ranging from your wardrobe choices or décor through writing prose or poetry or painting or sculpting. What makes you happy? What engages you? What takes you away from your day-to-day existence?

For some, cooking or entertaining may be creative outlets; childcare may bring out the creativity in others. You may garden or sing or dance or write wonderful letters or take photographs or crochet or sew or do crafts. How you express your creativity doesn't matter – it's that you find some creative outlet. Sara Eckel, in Come On! Be Creative!, written for Lifetime, has a wonderful list for unleashing your creativity: forget perfection; shush your inner critic; make room for inspiration, switch gears; use your downtime; and get busy. Just let loose!

What are you already doing that could be done in a more creative way? For example, could you find different activities to share with friends? My brother is part of a group that gets together monthly for a themed wine and appetizers evening.

One recent gathering centered around the game Clue. An aunt was in a group that tried out different cuisines for their monthly dinner. Some groups get together for a movie and a discussion. Others have book discussions.

Make a list of activities that you might want to change:

_____

_____

_____

_____

_____

_____

_____

_____

_____

_____

How Can You Find Outlets for Your Creativity?

Often, educational institutions and community organizations are a good place to start. Some continuing education programs have offerings targeted for creative expression, including languages, travel courses, cooking, painting, photography, needlework and jewelry design. Organizations like the Learning Annex are another great source. The YW/MCA and YW/MHA all offer a variety of programs. Film schools offer courses in acting, directing and film making for nonprofessionals as well as sponsoring lecture/movie review series. There are tour groups, many involving study or specialized activities like cooking classes, themed cruises and reading groups. Most craft supply and yarn stores offer classes and sponsor groups.

What appeals to you? Google it! You'll find countless ways to connect with others who share your passion face-to-face or virtually. No matter what you want to do, you can find other people to teach you or to join in with you.

Next Steps

How will you begin to explore your creativity?

_____

_____

_____

_____

_____

_____

_____

_____

_____

_____

_____

_____

Creativity/Self-expression Questions

Do I speak up for myself?

Do I take an active role in planning my own life?

What are the ways in which I can express myself?

How can family be a form of self-expression?

How do I want to express myself in my work?

What creative outlets do I want to develop?

How will I ensure time for self-expression?

Health and Wellness Blueprint Playbook

A step-by-step guide to remaining healthy in your ideal life

Health and Wellness

A man too busy to take care of his health is like a mechanic too busy to take care of his tools. Spanish Proverb

I don't care what anyone says – 60 is not the new 40. And your body will tell you so loud and clear unless you are paying careful attention to how you treat it. Our bodies do change. Our energy levels can change. This blueprint is about both the interior and exterior of your home. You can easily create a plan for yourself that keeps you feeling vibrant and healthy. You can even work to have a "real" age that is different than your chronological age.

How old are you now?

This is not about how many candles are on your birthday cake. There are many sites available to help you look at your lifestyle and calculate your age based on a variety of factors. The most popular one is www.realage.com. You can find a long list of other sites here: http://www.geriatricnursingcertification.com/blog/2008/whats-your-real-age-50-fun-fascinating-age-tests/.

Start designing your blueprint by using one of the resources above to find out how young you really are. That will help you focus on what should be in your plan moving forward.

Nutrition and Wellness

*Our bodies are our gardens – our wills
are our gardeners. William Shakespeare
An apple a day keeps the doctor away.
Anonymous*

It's sometimes easy to ignore the link between nutrition and practically everything else in life. Nutrition is an important part of the whole health picture. When you are suffering from the effects of stress, stick to a fresh, whole food diet that is high in complex carbohydrates, moderate in protein and low in fat. Reduce sugar to less that 2% of your diet and try to have that sugar come from fruit.

Be concerned with what you eat. Research shows that stress depletes our body of protein, B-vitamins, vitamin C and vitamin A. These can only be replaced and maintained through a well-balanced diet. Fruits and vegetables are excellent sources of vitamins, especially vitamin A (dark green vegetables and yellow vegetables such as carrots, squash, and sweet potatoes) and vitamin C (citrus fruits, peppers, baked potatoes, and strawberries).

Whole grains provide B-vitamins and iron. Fish, poultry, lean meats, dry beans and peas supply proteins. Dairy products are major sources of calcium and other nutrients. Good nutrition should also include supplements of vitamins and minerals, particularly B complex vitamins and vitamins A, C and E as well as selenium, calcium, magnesium among others. Take a multivitamin with high levels of calcium and vitamin D to support strong bones. Aim for 1,000 mg of calcium and about 600 IUs of vitamin D a day.

Avoid too many processed foods and foods high in fat, sugar and sodium. If possible, choose locally grown and organic products. Spend a little time reading labels on packaged foods to avoid nasty surprises.

Where and when you eat are very important. Avoid eating when you are in a hurry or unable to eat in a relaxing atmosphere. This affects your digestion as well as eating while driving, standing, talking on the telephone, working or doing something else at the same time you are eating. Avoid eating late at night.

Avoid emotional eating. Be aware of why you eat. Is it because you are hungry or because you are bored, depressed, anxious or need some kind of gratification? Do not use food as a Band-Aid. When you are under stress, chocolate bars, cookies and ice cream make you feel better initially, but you then gain weight that adds to your stress.

My Nutrition Plan

_____

_____

_____

_____

_____

_____

_____

_____

_____

_____

Physical Exercise

> *Physical fitness is not only one of the most important keys to a healthy body, it is the basis of dynamic and creative intellectual activity. John F. Kennedy*

Exercise is essential to a long and healthy life. As you age, muscle density decreases, so you may become weaker. Your metabolism starts to slow. Muscle fibers also become weaker and may be more prone to tearing during exercise or exaggerated movements. Blood vessel walls tend to harden. Exercise keeps blood vessels pliable. Light exercise also reduces the likelihood of diabetes, cancer, depression, dementia and even aging of the skin.

Exercise for at least 30 minutes per day. You don't have to live in the gym. Go for a walk. Dance in your living room – just get moving. Yoga is good for both mind and body and can range from gentle through strenuous. Consult with your doctor or experiment until you find something that's right for you.

The American College of Sports Medicine recommends aerobic exercise three to five days a week – 20 minutes of vigorous exercise or 30 minutes of moderate exercise. Include both stretching and strength training in your program to maintain muscle strength and flexibility.

Those who think they have no time for exercise will sooner or later have to find time for illness. Edward Stanley

My Physical Exercise Plan

_____

_____

_____

_____

_____

_____

_____

_____

_____

_____

Rest and Relaxation

Everything you do can be done better from a place of relaxation.
  Stephen C. Paul

Everyone needs balance. That means working hard, playing hard, laughing loud, and finding time to consciously detach and relax. Rest and relaxation are important parts of staying healthy and vital.

People who are happy tend to live longer than those who are unhappy.

Try to focus on the positive instead of the negative. Find things to laugh about. Laughter increases blood flow, boosts your immune system and releases endorphins. Avoid people who talk about illnesses to avoid getting caught up in a cycle of negativity. Avoid worrying. It won't help you solve your problem and it's not good for your health. Remember that most of the things that you worry about will probably never happen anyway.

> *Let us be of good cheer, remembering that the misfortunes hardest to bear are those which will never happen. James Russel Lowell*

Learn to meditate or find another techniques that calms you. Meditation reduces stress because it helps quiet your mind. Find a view or a picture that calms you and simply stare for a few minutes. Detach from your email, your cell phone and all other distractions. The one thing I find myself saying to my clients most often is, "Just breathe!" Spending 5 to 10 minutes per day practicing deep breathing reduces stress, relaxes your muscles, and improves your oxygen intake and delivery to all your organs and stimulate your lymphatic system.

Get enough sleep! You should sleep 6 to 8 hours per day to help your body replenish itself and rebuild its cells. Lack of sleep not only makes you feel tired but affects your eating habits. It's easy to mistake tiredness for hunger or to try to stay awake by loading up on high-sugar snacks.

Sleep studies show women experience more sleepless nights as they age. Develop a routine and stick to it as far as possible. Go to bed at the same time every night and get up at the same time every morning. Darken your bedroom. Light can keep you awake.

My Rest and Relaxation Plan

-1.

_____

_____

_____

_____

_____

_____

_____

_____

_____

_____

Mental Exercise

Keep your mind moving. Cognitive performance levels drop earlier in countries that have younger retirement age, according to a study published by the RAND Center for the Study of Aging and the University of Michigan. No, this doesn't mean that you should keep your job forever. There are many ways to keep your brain busy. Find activities that combine social, physical and intellectual stimulation.

Have a positive outlook. People who are positive tend to have better health and success in life then those who are negative. Appreciate your life, your health and whatever you have. Gratitude is good for your soul as well as your health. Set an intention to focus on things that make your life healthy and happy.

Do puzzles. Play games on your tablet or phone. Take a photography class. Travel – even if that simply means exploring neighborhoods in your own area. There are hidden treasures everywhere. You might find a small museum or a new restaurant or store. Find opportunities to engage in conversations.

My Mental Exercise Plan

-1.

_____

_____

_____

_____

_____

_____

_____

_____

_____

_____

Relationships

Surround yourself with friends and family members who are supportive. A research by Australian scientist suggested that people who have friends that they can count on to be there for them, live longer.

If you aren't close to – or don't really like – your family of birth, build a family of choice. Find communities of people with common interests. One of the best features of The Transition Network is their promotion of peer groups that bring together about ten women with common interests or simply geographic proximity or the same time free to meet.

My Relationship Plan

-1.

_____

_____

_____

_____

_____

_____

_____

_____

_____

_____

20 Tips for Managing Stress and Staying Healthy

1. Set realistic goals and do not expect to be perfect

In order to set realistic goals, you first have to create our own vision about life.

2. Become aware of your priorities in life

Take time to think about what makes you happy, what gives you joy and satisfaction in life.

3. Reevaluate your expectations

Stress is sometimes the difference between your expectations and reality. You will experience less stress when you realize and accept that everything in this world is always changing, that nothing holds still and that you face new challenges every day. And guess what? You have no control over this, so learn to accept there are things you cannot change and if you fight them you will experience a lot of stress.

4. Schedule time for yourself and keep the appointment

Let's start with your daily schedule. You should be able to find at least 10 or 15 minutes every day to be alone with your thoughts. Insulate yourself from telephone calls, beepers, computers or other stress producing equipment and replenish yourself. Do meditation, visualization, self-massage, relaxation. We will discuss these techniques later on.

5. Discover ways to share your stress and constructively express your emotions

Do you know that according to health researchers, counseling can reduce the risk of a heart attack ? It helps to talk to someone about your concerns and worries. Another person can help you see your problems in a different light. There are times, if you feel your problem is serious, when you need professional help; there are other times when all you need is to talk to a friend, but the main idea here is that you need to let it out. How you do it depends on the severity of your troubles and your ability to handle the situation, but the important thing is that you need to talk about it. It is important to note that knowing when to ask for professional help may avoid more serious problems later.

6. Free yourself from anger

Whether you want to admit it or not, you have felt or still feel angry at someone or something. Anger is one of main sources of stress. It is a very anxiety-provoking feeling and difficult to get rid of. You think that if you forget, whatever or whoever made you angry is going to make you angry again. I still do not know whether the answer is to forget or not, but I am convinced that you need to forgive and at the same time you could still learn from the experience

7. Develop and maintain a network of caring people

Solitude is important, but you also need to feel connected with other people in life. I do not mean just having a lot of friends with whom you go out and have fun. I am talking of people, men or women, with whom you develop the kind of understanding that only comes from a deep sharing of experiences. This means people with whom you can break your silence about certain emotional issues in your life, people who helps you uncover your hidden fears. These relationships help you define who you really are and more important, they give true meaning to your life.

8. Use your emotions

Have a good cry if you feel like it. Crying helps us cope with powerful emotions, negative or positive, and according to scientists it also helps us get rid of chemicals in our bodies created by moments of stress. Hold on to your sense of humor. A good laugh can get you through the worst of times.

9. Approach problems as challenges

The following steps may help you :

Ask yourself in a very objective manner: What is it that I have to face? Define your challenge.

Make a list of the individuals or situations associated with the situation.

Make a list of the decisions you could make to face the challenge.

Think of the resources or people that may help you face the challenge.

Develop a strategy and put it into action. Remember, do not give up until a solution is reached!

10. Listen to your mind

Please, give yourself time to expose yourself to yourself. If you learn to focus on what you are doing and not only on its content, you may find that unexpected personal feelings will come to the surface. This will help you increase your awareness of what is going on in your life. When you decide to do this, it could be your best day or the worst. It could lead to confusion, guilt or shame. However, it could be the beginning of an emotionally healthier life.

11. Listen to your body (small aches and pains), especially when you are pushing too hard

You may try to lie to yourself but your body is more honest. When you feel too tired, have a headache, feel pain in our neck or back, your body is trying to send you a message. In some cases, it may be telling you that you are under more emotional stress than you can take. In other words, you have gone beyond your comfort zone.

12. Interrupt the stress through time-outs

Mini-breaks can make all the difference. Marsha goes to the beach when her job begins to get to her. She never leaves her desk – she just focuses her thoughts on a favorite vacation spot for a minute or two and comes back refreshed. Karen takes a walk. Even a trip to the ladies' room is enough to break the stress cycle.

13. Write empowerment statements

Eliminate "cannot," instead choose "I will." Choose an affirmative statement and make it a part of your life. Post this affirmative statement in your home and/or office. Post it in a place where you will see it every day.

14. Be a good friend to yourself

Examine the way you treat yourself. If you don't treat yourself well, how can you expect others to treat you well? Remind yourself that you are a worthwhile person. Learn to be patient with yourself.

15. Develop your own definition of success

In order to do this, you have to get rid of preconceived notions to get to your underlying truth. In other words, to find out what type of person you really are, what it is that you really want out of life. Remember we all have our own truth and are unique way to see the world, this is what you must reach for, not somebody else's version.

16. Organize yourself and learn to manage your time

Make a regular schedule of activities you enjoy. It is good to organize yourself, but make plans for fun along the way. Decide what makes you happy and make time to do it. Do not answer the telephone during meals. Learn to say no. Get rid of people or things you do not love or like

17. Clutter causes chaos; chaos leads to stress.

When you can't find things, your stress level can begin to rise. Think of all the time you lose trying to remember where you put something. Similarly, too many people in your life demanding attention creates a kind of chaos and limits the amount of quality time you can spend with those you love.

18. Simplify your life.

Get rid of anything in your space that you do not love or do not use. If you are surrounded by a few things that you love, you have time to enjoy them. If you can easily find the things that you need to use, you will operate more efficiently. Be equally ruthless with your relationships. Spend your time with people who nourish and replenish you. Help and support them and let them help and support you.

19. Don't neglect your spiritual life.

Seek meaning and purpose in life. Create some quiet time for meditation or prayer. Experiment with soothing music. Nurture hobbies that help you express yourself and renew your spirit.

20. Have fun.

Get silly. Giggle. Watch bad movies – whatever it takes to insert a little glee into your life.

Notes

Bettina Aptheker. (1989) Tapestries of Life: Women's Work, Women's Consciousness, and the Meaning of Daily Experience. University of Massachusetts Press. Amherst, MA

Dr. Gene Cohen. (2001) The Creative Age. Harper Collins.

Tori DeAngelis Women at Midlife.
http://www.naswdc.org/diversity/women/032503.asp

Sara Eckel. Come On! Be Creative!. Lifetimetv.com: Health - Come On, Be Creative!

Kathy English. The Healing Power of Female Friendships.   http://www.freshjuice.ca/be-well/disease-prevention/the-healing-power-of-female-friendships/a/39412

Deb Gebeke . (1990) Family Stress: Changes and Challenges. NDSU Extension Service, North Dakota State University

Mardy Ireland (1993). Reconceiving Women: Separating Motherhood from Female Identity. The Guilford Press.

Robert L. Rubinstein, Baine B. Alexander, Marcene Goodman, and Mark Luborsky. (1991) .. Journal of Gerontology. September; 46(5): S270–S277

Karen Springen and Sam Seibert. (2005) *Don't ever assume your best work is behind you.* Newsweek.

Paula J. Wart. (2006) Stella Henry with Ann Convery The Eldercare Handbook. *The healing power of female friendships*,

Dana Wilson the Child Welfare League of America, kinship care.
http://www.cwla.org/programs/kinship/faq.htm

Acknowledgements

So many people contribute to any project, and this is true of this book. Life Blueprints grows out of a lifelong interest in learning and helping women grow. Dr. Mary Sue Richardson nurtured my interest in Women's Studies while I was studying at NYU. My students in the Cooperative Education program at Medgar Evers College taught me the value of life history as the basis for career exploration. Dr. Jack Mezirow guided my dissertation work on self-esteem in women and introduced me to transformative learning. Strive's LIFFT program gave me the opportunity to test and revise much of the material that appears in this book and taught me wonderful lessons in the strength and courage of women. I am grateful for all these teachers.

Friends and family have supported this project in so many ways – listening, just being there, reading materials. Betsy Mickel was my wonderful editor. Jim Meyer provided endless internet support. My wonderful coaches, Donna Steinhorn and Natalie

Tucker Miller have been both cheerleaders and shoulders to cry on as needed. Finally, I want to thank everyone who has ever attended one of my workshops and everyone who picks up a copy of this book.

Let me know what you think of the book or get in touch if you'd like to be coached by me.
Susan R. Meyer

www.susanrmeyer.com

About the Author

I'm in the business of creating happy endings. That's because my life has been the stuff fairy tales are made of. My mother died before I was nine and my easy-going father married the prototypical wicked stepmother. She was emotionally distant and physically abusive, and finally sent me off to Grandmother's house, where I learned to cope with the resident Big Bad Wolf - my abusive alcoholic grandfather. I spent years hiding and being quiet at home while being myself and building strength at school. When I was thirteen, my father died and I began to figure out that I needed to be my own Prince Charming and create all the good things I wanted in life on my own. All this makes me a great coach. I know how to help you create what you want – whether it's a totally different life or a few tweaks, whether it's leadership skills or retirement planning. I can help you see into your crystal ball and build on what's revealed.

I've coached women returning to work, managers wanting to be happier and more productive, people who felt like failures or had no self-confidence and successful women who wanted just a little bit more in their lives. I have a doctorate in Adult Education and Leadership, from Teachers College, Columbia University, and master's degrees in Educational Psychology and Counseling from New York University. I am an IAC Certified Coach and Board Certified Coach. My *Women Living for Today and Tomorrow* workshops were featured in The New York Times.

Find out more about me at www.susanrmeyer.com.

www.ingramcontent.com/pod-product-compliance
Lightning Source LLC
LaVergne TN
LVHW051253080426
835509LV00020B/2952